ESCAPE
From the endless war

Hiabu Hassebu

Scriptor House LLC

2810 N Church St Wilmington, Delaware, 19802

www.scriptorhouse.com

Phone: +1302-205-2043

Published by Scriptor House LLC

Paperback ISBN: 979-8-88692-158-8

eBook ISBN: 979-8-88692-159-5

ACKNOWLEDGMENTS

Thanks for my creative mind to conclude with 5. I'm grateful to Mark Zuckerberg, who created face book, to entertain my busy mind. My gratitude, to my conservative mother, Hansu and libertarian father, Hassebu. Above all, thanks to Sibhat Tadesse, who willingly assisted me, in all life issue. I've testimony, and my gratitude goes, to Dr. Alganesh Gandi, Mrs. Meron Estifanos and Reverend Father Musie Zerai, who really are struggling to save lives, by involving in the situation of the Eritrean and other African refugees.

ABOUT THE AUTHOR

Here's the author, if you rally want, to know him. He's born, at the time, when Radio access, was at its pick and TV broadcasting was black and white.

I was born when tradition was respected, to its maximum level and the attitude of surprise was practiced, day by day. No monogram, no foretelling of the sex, just a surprise.

I don't tell, my birthday and the year, to let my readers guessing. I was just born, where social facts count and the religious attitude was followed.

I don't mention, either, where I came from, but I assure you, I'm from the same planet. You might be eager, to know my gender, but my libertarian mind, won't allow me so.

I'm writing, in the times, of the male centered, historical narrations and tales as they're fading.

I was born, when the speed of innovation, was every twenty years. Not to be fortunate, right now I'm struggling, in the middle of the Digital era.

One who wakes up early, commands. For those who come late, there're two chances, either to win or lose. If I'm to chose, I chose the early risers.

No need to go to a library, when all's in Google. No need to go to the cinema, when You-tube is there. No need to locate an address, when GPS, is in hand.

Don't worry, in the end, when you cover my script, reading, you'll figure out three things, my name, my age and gender.

Still, I persist on my own doing, despite the unwanted resistances. It's not easy, as one would think of. My mind's still back home, and I'm here in the USA, unable, to promote my reality, to be someone, in the land of prosperity. To function and adapt to this life, is hard to imagine. "All things function, but no one, lives a true life" my mind says in silence.

I wandered into many things. In two decades, I covered a lot of them, if you allow me to recite some of them. The very day, I landed on the soil of the USA, was for a reason of my master's studies. My student status lasts there, while I was in Chicago. My status rejected. Caught in between being deported or exist differently. I never wanted to lose my future. Struggled for decades as

UN documented. In 2008 my first book came out, into the scene of Americans.

Made my mind to get revised my status, as I send my book, to a special sector of immigration department. There I was accepted. Got my green card in three weeks.

Mr. International they call me, as people see me interacting, in four European languages and another four East-African languages.

I bought your book, I need you to autograph for me, he says, a gentle man, who comes every Tuesday, for a delivery inventory. His name's Mr. Dave. When ever he sees me he calls me, "Mr. Professor". He always, wanted to chat with me. Our chats, at times are political, current affair and cross- cultural exchanges. His eagerness, to know about Africa, made our relation better. One day he raises a question, on how to deal, with the unification of Africa as one nation. "It's not easy", I say. "Why?" he asks. "For reasons of the outside influences", I respond. He nods.

Poetry's the field I very much handle good, since my childhood. I used to recite, a self composed poems, in my mother language, "Tigryna". Here's one of the poem, enjoy it.

"Be free and then"....

Be free and then act.

Be free and then react.

Be free and then comment

. Be free and then reflect

. Be free and then judge.

Be free and then charge.

Be free and then claim.

Be free and then blame.

Be free and then discuss

. Be free and then refuse.

Be free and then instruct

. Be free and then distract

. Be free and then condemn

. Be free and then confirm

. Be free and then propose.

Be free and then depose

. For it's in being free, the simple mind agree, to deal with life,

in all its struggle strife.

"Enough!"...with

"Who I'm"....

DEAR READERS.

It took me several tries, to get into how to name the script and come with a title.

My mind finally landed, to give my narratives a specific tone and quality. "An Escape: from an Indefinite war", I titled it, to recount the horrible experience of the locals war tragedies.

The beats and hits I use, leans towards the real life, a novel based on a true experience.

Basically, my narration is in present tens and my style's defined by four main characters. It all goes, with the two female Freedom fighters, Anna and Asli, with their respective kids, Sami and Saba. The particular issue, I wanted to articulate, is about the theme of war and revolution.

The story I tell, is right now happening. Cleared myself, the story to be a novel. The name mentioning is random. If in case, there's anything, I'm here to defend myself.

PROLOGUE

I heard a voice telling me from above, I guess heaven. "Here you go". This is the independence, you were waiting for more than a quarter of a century. "Do you like it like this"? If you do so enjoy it.

It's the voice of one of the martyrs.

"Alright" I say, though I'm a little bit distracted by the vision. Then, I look to the right and left. My eyes can see, only the locals, wearing their traditional festive vestment, rambling on the street.

The country is, in celebration of its Independence, after 30 years of armed struggle. The devastating long war, has reduced and drained the normal life of the locals. The joy and happiness they are experiencing, is an imaginable. People are on the streets celebrating.

Home discipline, for the time being is forgotten. No one is at home. I can't believe it. This seems to energize my soul, not to recite, the same story of affliction. But I don't know what and how to tell. I still can't bring, myself, to tell about the reality, the reality of joy and happiness, the locals are experiencing.

"Look at these" I say, feeling excited about the situation.

"No, I don't have anything against celebrating."... "It won't help either." Agreed to the situation, my mind announces.

"I'm looking at the situation emotionally." I urged simply delighted.

Zaku, an elder Freedom fighter sees it realistically. My mother intervenes.

"Slavery is gone once for all" she shouts.

Zaku, looks at me sharply, again back to my mother.

He sighs, in his mind revisiting the life in the revolution, where he was involved for three decades.

"Still nothing to say?" says Mom, stepping towards the kitchen leaving us on our own.

I pushed to follow his remarks, seriously. "What's the fear? I asked.

He sighs, "Well, don't get me wrong, but I'm sensing the condition of the independence, differently."

I gaze at his face, mildly smiling.

"For me it's too early to celebrate", he says, breathing deep. "Naturally, the salt should dissolve, to make the food tasty", he expresses, sensing a thaw.

I didn't want to enter, into what he's feeling. At the same I can't ask about his past experience in the revolution.

He makes a move. "You see, it'll be tough, for the revolution, to dissolve in its own people.

Though my mind didn't agree that time, after ten years, I saw it through my eyes.

"I sigh", connecting the dots of yesterday to current peoples life. For eight years, things have been functioning, along normally for the people. Then in 1998 a war broke between Eritrea and Ethiopia. The new Constitution is dumped and trashed. The jungle rule substituted it. The reign of the dictatorship's on its rise. The military services became dominant. As it became the service for UN definite time, the youth generation began, to run out of it, by escaping in masses.

I laughed without a reason, as my mind repeats, the political slogan. "In few years the country is going to be like a Singapore", it says. My mind clashed with the reality, without knowing precisely, what made this hysterical.

My mind failed to compare. Several years later, my sympathy faded out, let alone to be the Singapore of Africa, years in and out, it was listed at the last, the tail of the world progress.

I wouldn't tell you what you want to hear. I feel politically correct, if that's acceptable. When the entire, democracy seekers, (The G15), the journalists, and other faith groups are suffering, jailed in a fox-hole or man made containers; When the youth generation, are deserting the country, to end up either on the Sahara desert, or drowned in the Sea; When all known business owners, escape their land to live in other African countries; "It's ridiculous" I voiced, and really it's ridiculous, even to recount it. If I'm to proceed, reciting, the hostile attitude of the regime, it's very painful, full-stop, Enough.

Here goes the story....

THE BEGINNINGS.

This's important. Saba's in my mind. In addition to being my best friend, also she's my comrade in the armed struggle for the Independence of the nation.

It happened while both on the trench, standing side by side, fighting against the enemy. The weather is cloudy. The visibility was to none. A cold wind mixed with a mist rain drops makes it more difficult to see the enemy.

A bullet breaks through her forehead. As she falls on the ground, raises her fist up on the air, pronouncing "Victory for the masses", she passes away. I call her name "Saba!

Saba!" yelling. Then I scream, as if calling her by name, was to save her life. I'll never forget that day, the day of her sacrifice.

Three days before the Independence, the Eritrean liberation army, surprised the enemy's last defensive trenches. After an intense and heavy fighting, they were able to break the front of Dekamhare and march towards the Capital city Asmara.

That day.

The eve of the Independence day, Anna is on her way waiting for a lift, sitting on a small rock, facing towards a river bank of Anseba. She looks tired and exhausted of all the walk. She pulls her little battery radio and follows the Radio of "Dimtsi Hafash" (Voice of the masses).

There was not news besides a continued, non-stop revolutionary songs. Weariness rolled over her head.

Asli walks down the street to join with Anna at the river bank. When Asli reaches her, she loudly calls Anna's name. Her voice sounded, like it was coming, from the mountain tips. Asli, sits beside her on a rock.

"What happened with you, Anna?" Asli asks.

"Have you heard any news?" responds Anna, backfiring with a question.

"Well, I know you're upset..." Asli says, closing her eyes, in seconds to open it.

"I'm not upset but concerned", responds, breathing of let it go.

Anna sighs.

"Even this things are going to pass" says, Anna, her ears fixed with the radio, listening the monotonous songs, emitted from Sahel mountains.

Asli, quietly leans towards her.

"What things? She asks, giving Anna, a sideways glance.

"Oh nothing personal." She responds, thinking briefly about the no news situation.

"I'm still in the old issue", Anna says, obviously feeling confused about the war situation.

Asli glances at her quickly. "Still there with the old issue?"..." I mean the yesterday issue, we both were involved with".

Anna "nods". "Good guess", she agrees.

Asli, sighs. "I'm getting worried". She says, taking a moment to cool her down.

"Too early to complain about the new issue", she adds.

Anna takes a deep breath. "I'm still bothered more about the new issue."

"The new issue!" Asli demands, waving her hand dismissively". "By the way, can you say something about it", she asks raggedly.

Anna shrugs.

Keeps silent for seconds, thinking of anything to say.

"Just to start life, all over again, as civilians", Anna voices.

Asli bits her lips.

"Do you see anything I don't see?" "Hush", Anna whispers.

"Do you really want to know?". "Yes"... Asli nods.

"The whole time we spent, in the revolution",... pauses Anna, for seconds closing her eyes.

Anna, struggles back into a sitting position. Asli, flicks on the sun's light staring at herself. "So"... Asli responds, staring at Anna.

"Our life, a military style one",... "culturally will clash with the life of our simple people".

"I hear you"...but it's too early to complain.

AND NOW

A nine months pregnant, Anna, nicknamed "Mortar", is about to give birth, to her first daughter.

"Hurry, lets take her to the nearest Hospital", shouts, the driver of military truck, comrade Sultan. Load her, at the back, with a female fighter Asli, nicknamed "Fenji", to assist her.

"Comrade!"... "give it more gas, to reach at least, the nearest clinic"... "if not the main hospital", shouts, Asli, who is sitting at the back.

"Ok, I'm trying my best, despite the ugly road, slowing me down", responds the Driver, grinning so fiercely.

Anna's groaning tone, picks to its highest tone.

"Keep up, your sense of morality as a fighter", Asli, yelled over the ugly groan of Anna.

The engine howls to its maximum speed. Sultan, turns his face towards Bini, who is sitting besides him.

"Our rush, might result to another unexpected result", says Sultan, whispering, leaning against his ear.

"What do you mean by that?" Responds Bini, waiting for his response.

"I mean she might give birth, before we reach our destination, the Hospital" responds Sultan.

"I imagine, with this speed anything could happen",... "you said it yourself", not bothering to agree.

"What can we do, if it ever happens, we don't have the maternity experience, to do it ourselves", asks Bini.

"I hear you", the only training we got is, how to shoot.

"I mean, if there're no horses to pull the cart, the donkeys are available", he says, rolling his eyes.

Confused about his say, he waits a few seconds, to give him his explanation.

"You see",... "if the professional care givers, are not available, we can do something",...

"To mean what?" asks Sultan.

" I mean to handle the delivery". Bini responds.

Another big and loud groan is heard. "Lessen the speed please", Bini advices.

Asli, is still struggling to assist Anna. It's the last groan, before the delivery. The lucky baby, is self delivered on the way, before reaching the destination.

"Stop! Stop the car", shouts Asli, from the back.

Sultan, abruptly, stops, by pressing hardly, the stop pad.

"The baby is already out, already breathing the air of our planet", shouts out, Asli, trying to wrap up, the crying baby, by her cloth.

All start to chat, about the sudden delivery. Asli, smiles at Anna and the new baby.

"Since, you own the right to choose name",... "what name will you give, to the baby?", Asli asks.

Anna, looks at her, offering her a mild smile. Asli, makes her eyes narrow.

"Say it, say it, if ever you have one", repeats Asli, trying to keep up the joy, with a smile.

"Don't push me, to say it now",... says Anna taking a deep breath.

Anna shot back, "you know our culture", gazing at her sideways.

Asli shrugs her thin shoulders. Asli squeezes her hand.

"There's a name giving day and I better prefer, to wait the day"....

Asli smiles.

"I mean, it's not like I'm blind, or obvious to the culture" Asli responds, not to challenge her.

"To bake or not, first let's reach the water", Anna expresses in a say.

Asli winces.

"I like your say", Asli says after being silent for seconds. "I prefer to say nothing.... Anna says, bowing her head down. Asli smiles back.

"I hope you don't take it personal", Anna says, lifting her head up.

Both scowled at their upper body, in silence.

After several miserable minutes, Sultan, hurries over driving fast, down the twisted rough road. Bini is wondering, by the unexpected delivery of Anna. He smiles at Sultan, gazing at him sideway.

"How far is the nearest clinic?" asks Bini. "It's half a mile drive", responds Sultan. He gets frustrated of the rough drive.

"What a lousy day!" Bini says, breathing out deep. Anna, groans softly to herself.

"I feel thirsty",... "any water around here?" Anna asks. Asli, searches down the trucks floor.

Asli frowns. "No".

Bini, finds a bottle of water under his seat. Hands, the bottle to Asli.

He stuck his head through the window, looking at the side mirror.

Asli hands the bottle to Anna. Anna grabs the bottle, looks at her, her eyebrows raised. "Quench you thirsty", Asli says. Anna, after drinking half bottle, opens her eyes wide.

"Asli, I know you're honest", Anna says, licking her lips. Asli nods.

"You, been always besides me", she ads. Asli, thought about her say for a minute.

"It's not me but the revolution taught me", responds, without mentioning their life, as freedom fighters.

CLINIC.

Five minutes later, they reach the nearest clinic, at the suburb of the capital city. Sultan, parks the car, alongside of the parking lot. Looks back.

"Finally we did it", he says, forwarding his smile to Anna and Asli, who are waiting to be let out.

Bini, opens the backdoor. Both step out, with the new baby, carried by Asli. Asli, turns her face to both.

"Thank you". She says. In a weak voice.

"Thank you for helping me" says, Anna.

"Sure, I do hope, she gets to feeling better", responds, Sultan.

In a slow motion, Anna and Asli, walk towards the clinic.

"Come on Anna, you always been a strong woman", says Asli, looking her slow motion of steps. Anna, follows her inside the clinic, instantly, to fall her body, on one of the benches, attempting to sit down.

With the baby in her hand, Asli, steps towards the receptionist desk. The female Clerk, smiles at her. The baby starts to cry, loudly. To calm the baby, she lightly, waves the baby, left and right. It stops crying.

The Clerk smiles.

"Is it your baby?" she asks.

"No ma'am", Asli says, turning her face, towards Anna. The Clerk looks at Anna side way.

"The one who is sitting, who's she?" Asks the Clerk. "A Freedom fighter!" Asli respond confidently".

"Oh, a Freedom fighter!" the Clerk voices, in a lower tone.

"How may I help you? Asks the Clerk, blinking her eyes, for seconds.

After copying, the needed information, leads them to a bedroom.

The Clerk, goes back out, heading towards the main office, on her way in the middle of the corridor, to meet with a Nurse. The Nurse's, all out in her white uniform.

"How's the new patient? Asks the Nurse, waiting for seconds, for her response.

"She's fine",... "I just set them a room, to stay in".

The Nurse, proceeds walking down the corridor, heading towards the patients room. At the threshold, meets Asli, who is standing in the middle of the door.

"Are you the patient?" Asks the Nurse politely.

"I'm just assisting, but the Patient is there, lying on the bed" Asli responds.

Walks in and greets Anna. Steps near the bed and focuses on Anna. The baby is gorgeously sleeping.

"Cute baby!" exclaims, as she smiles, to Anna. "Your first baby? Again asks.

Anna nods.

"I guess, you weren't assisted, by our staff, am I right?" She asks.

"Yes ma'am" Anna nods.

"I wouldn't just be peering into your personal life" she smiles.... "But it's my duty to ask questions".... "Bare with me".

Takes out a note-book, from her files and sits around a small desk, to proceed with her personal questioning.

"Are you, in a position, to answer to my questions? Anna, "Nods".

"Okay, make yourself comfortable", she says, smiling. "What's your name?" she asks, staring with a smile. "Anna" she responds, returning her a smile.

"Wow beautiful name." She says blinking with a smile. "Work please?" looking at her face with attention. "A Fighter." Anna responds.

"You mean fire fighter? "Not exactly".

"So what?"

"A Freedom fighter". Very interesting I really couldn't stop my excitement.

"Why?"

"My male-centered mind is set to accept",... "only men are Freedom fighters.

"Now you know", "seen is believing". "I agree".

The Nurse, looks at her expectantly. "I thought we'd do a medical questioning?"

"Alright!" Anna, nods, trying not to smile. "When where you born?"

"The year the revolution started". "You mean, 1961?"

"Correct".

Rests her head back in her pillow.

"I'm sorry, for all of my questioning?"... "I see, your physical weakness".... "I won't hold you further".

"The reason you are here please?" Shakes her head in disbelieve.

"I myself am surprised of my being here". "Oh, I feel a bit confused."

"It's not my choice to be here, either".

"There's no point, proceed with my questioning", she says, definitely trying to make a turn, not to question her more.

"Go, have some fun with your questioning" says Anna, seeming very comfortable.

"Maybe, I shouldn't", pauses for seconds.

"'To make it short, I'm here for further medical assistance" Anna reacts, blinking her eyes.

"To your excitement"...The Nurse looks at her.

"I've something to tell you",... "I delivered my baby, while on the way".

Interrupts her in the middle. "Really"...

"Hang on, did you say, you delivered on the street? Sighs. "Yes but inside a truck".

"I can tell, in your voice".... "I'm in shock, you delivered your baby, this way" she responds, sort of getting perplexed.

"I'm also shocked on how to explain to you, either", giving her a quick look".... "You don't doubt. Do you?

"No, I don't" the Nurse smiles back, giving her one last, lost look.

"I've had a long talk, with you,"... "for now let's close our discussion".... "It's great, you've finally done it" she says getting amused.

DOCTORS OFFICE.

The Nurse, gets out of the room and steps towards the Doctor's office, walking down the hall. The office door, is half open, and he sitting on a chair, wearing his white gown. She steps in with all files in her hand. She smiles a wide smile.

"I see you, wandering from room to room, though it's part of your job", he says, lightly laughing.

"I hope you're not serious about that", she smiles.

"I'm not kidding you, please sit down, I'm ready to listen to you" he says, looking at her in between his eye glasses.

"I have something to tell you, Doctor" she says, attempting to sit down.

"A new or an old version?" "New", she responds.

"Go ahead", he says, anxiously waiting to hear about the news.

"The new patient, she is a Freedom fighter. He nods humbly.

"How did you find, that she is a Freedom fighter?

"It just came up in our discussion".... "I've hardly even figured out, in our long discussion".... "What made me to be surprised more, she delivered a baby girl, on her way".

"God is good". He giggles. In his mind, thinking, half of the job is done. For a second, the Nurse actually looks at the Doctor, in the eye.

"I think I'm curious, you know".... "I can't have you serving your patient, like that".

"I'm sorry", he smiles, shaking his head.

Asli, who's patiently waiting, at the waiting room, steps back towards the room. Anna, jumps from her bed, when she sees her, walking through the door.

Puts her finger to her lips. "What happen?" Asli, asks.

"Nothing", Anna responds, looking so upset.

"You know her approach, I didn't like it".... "She didn't sound like a nurse".... "She almost drained my mind, with litany of questions, one after the other, that I can't handle".

"You remember?" Asli, interrupts her. "Remember what?" She ventures.

Pauses for seconds...." The very day, when we first joined the liberation front".

Anna, sighs.

"The trainer cadre, to rain us with many questions", she says, her mind running through the old armed resistance.

"That's different story and different discipline, Anna responds, holding up her palm.

"I don't want to remember, that either", Asli sighs. "I hope I'm not right", she adds.

Almost an hour later, the Nurse, after discussing enough with the Doctor in his office, she steps towards Anna's room. She approaches both, standing still in the middle of the room.

Anna and Asli follow her, not saying anything, in silence. She leans towards Anna, glancing with a smile at her face.

"You're in good shape", the Nurse says, shooting at her, a joyous look. A long pause. Finally, the Nurse ventures.

"Well", Anna you'll be discharged and soon you'll be home" she says.

"I can't wait to see, Mom, Dad, my brothers and sisters, says, a smile coming back on to her face.

Asli, sighs. "The same feeling, at least we're lucky, to be alive".

Anna, steps towards her baby's bed. Raises her up to her chest, kissing her repeatedly.

"I can't stop thanking God, for getting the baby girl",... "Your name will be "Saba".... "To hold on, my favorite Comrade, martyr, a hero female fighter, for the Independence".

Enters, into a deep thought, reciting in her memory, the up and down of the armed struggle.

Sighs.

"At last, the awful war is terminated.... "How many young freedom fighters, passed away, by being sacrifice, not to see the independence.

1991 May 24.

Loud voices of shout, are heard at large, on the main street of the capital city, Asmara. All eyes dart toward the window.

"You see, the whole city is on the street", says Asli, just staring at her face.

"Our people have the reason to celebrate", says Anna, glancing at her.

The Nurse, walks towards the room. The door is open, but for a reason of courtesy, she, lightly knocks the door. Steps in. Innocent smile shining on her face, greets them.

"Freedom fighters, the liberators of the land", she says, flashing her eyes to the ceiling.... "The loud shout of joy, you are just hearing",... "is because of your sacrifice", she says, backing her say, how much she means it.

"No sense of bragging", responds Asli.

"Everyone paid the price, you in town and us on the field", Anna says, exhaling out her breath deep.

"But still I stand curious, all in all about the revolution",... "the armed struggle, you are part of" the Nurse, repeats....

"How did it work for you to be part of it? She adds.

Anna, as a freedom fighter, wants to prove herself, launching to the reality of it.

"I'm glad that this worrisome war, finishes there once and for all"....

Gets her focus together.

"You see, the fighting stuff, I don't want to do it anymore, says Anna.

Three days later.

Anna is not in bed, when the Nurse, walks in. She is sitting, in the veranda on a wooden chair. The city is quiet. The euphoria of the independence celebrant is doomed. Summer, is in its early days. No fans' no ACs, to refresh the room, with cool air. Anna, looks back the room, through the tiny window glass. The Nurse steps towards the baby's bed. The baby is struggling to breath the hot air. Non-stop she cries. The Nurse picks her up.

"My God! Where's her mother",... "leaving the baby, on her own, says, raising her voice.

"That's crazy!" Doing something dangerous as that.

Anna, steps in. The Nurse narrows her eyes, and confronts her.

"Don't you think, it's crazy idea, to leave your baby, on her own?, Asks.

"I do",... "I was just out for a while" Anna adds...." I couldn't resist the heat at all", she says, as she goes quiet.

In seconds, Anna responds. "I'm sorry", blinks her eyes, by my negligence, to turn it into an argument.

Asli, steps towards the room. When she sees Anna, in solitude, silently busy with her mind, intervenes to distract her.

"You sound upset?" Don't you? Asli asks. "I do!"... "Mrs. Mind reader", she answers.

"I wish, I was a martyr, like my husband", Anna says, drawing in a breath.

The Nurse, shows up in the middle of their discussion. "A Freedom fighter and now a Mom",... "get ready",... "in one hour time you'll be discharged from our clinic".

"We hear you", Asli responds, squinting her eyes.

"Everyone, is enjoying the independence, because of you",... "I mean your sacrifice", the Nurse says, glancing at both, with a wide smile.

Asli, walks outside in the dark, all the way to the Taxi stop. Walks, down the main road, looking right and left, to see, of any available taxi, is on the road.

Ten minutes, later as she is sitting and waiting, a yellow taxi, comes after while. Raises, from where she's sitting, waving her hands up.

The Taxi driver, instantly stops. Gets in, takes the window seat, at the back and drive heading, towards the clinic.

Anna, is already out waiting, few blocks up from the entrance of the clinic. The taxi driver, stops in the middle, parking alongside the road. Flashes, yellow lights in the dark.

Asli, opens the back door and steps towards Anna. "Come on!... "The taxi is here", yelling on the air.

Anna, with her baby, steps towards the taxi. The driver, starts the motor again.

"Your destination pleas", he asks, driving real slow.

"AderAda" says Asli, mentioning the name of a village, 18 kilometers distant, from the capital city.

"Not my route",... "you better take a bus", he says. Anna and Asli, don't answer for seconds, looking at each other in distress.

"By the way you don't look civilian? Am I right? He asks, looking through the rearview.

"Right guess",... "but if we aren't civilian, what do you think we are? Asli responds, frowning.

"I feel glad to host you in my Taxi",... "I mean it's for the first time to meet female Freedom fighters", he says, calculating his say. Both smile an innocent smile, while he's eager, to follow them silently. There's a pause. Anna yawns, looking up the taxi's ceiling.

Then she says quickly. "You know what?"

His mind stuck, stammering.

"The armed struggle, for the independence, have socially divided, our people, in to two categories, Anna says, feeling uncomfortable about the revolution's indoctrination.

"What do you mean by that?" He asks.

"I mean it really created, two different thoughts, in one social life", Asli, intervenes,... "you see, we're both caught by our experience",... "right now as we speak".

He joins, to her idea to a certain level, while waiting for her explanation.

"The dual social expression, between "Gebar" (civil servant) and "Tegadelti", (Freedom fighters), will totally destroy, our social fabric as people.

After half an hour drive, the Taxi driver turns right, towards the village, flashing his light. At the next corner, he stops. Goes down, stepping towards the backdoor, to open the door.

"I would be very glad to see you again", he smiles "Y o u r ride is free", he says, again smiling joyfully

"Anyway thank you", he says, rising his right and waving on the air. Both wave their hands, as he drives backward in reverse.

Anna's Village.

Both keep walking, deep into the village, crossing house after house. On their way, in the near distant, they hear a church bell ringing.

Asli, picks the baby up. "The revolution life is like a religious life".

Anna, giggles, "do you mean, a life without Angels?

"That's right",… "a struggle, to level of giving oneself, as a sacrifice", responds.

After a brief pause, Anna starts, to revise the conversation earlier they had, with the Taxi driver.

"We had good time, with the Taxi driver, haven't we?" Anna voices in whisper tone.

"Of course!" Asli responds, agreeing to her view.

"I hope we told our story, like they really happen", Anna says,… "but I've fear, that our people might compare us with the Angels", she sighs.

"That's my fear too", says Asli, staring at Anna. "But my fear's, that our social belongings, might lose its sense.

The testing time, of a guiltless female Freedom fighter, starts right from here. Asli, with the baby on her chest, following Anna, they walk deep to the village. Suddenly, Anna stops and freezes standing, as she sees her family house is entirely demolished. Walks, few steps towards the demolished house.

Anna's, Grandpa and Grandma are in their earlier 90. Grandpa, in his youth age, he's been forcefully recruited as "Ascari" in the Italian military. He fought in three big battles, that of Kesela, Barentu and Keren against the British military.

How much did you enjoy, by being Italian soldier? She asks. You're getting funny, I guess, he says, not clearly embarrassed by her say. Looks, lonesome and worried about the war situation, though, feels consoled, by the success of the freedom fighters, to liberate the whole country.

"I hope to see, Anna, our grand daughter, safe and alive", he says coughing hard.

"We never know, but we have to expect the good and bad, responds Grandma, staring at his face.

"Let's wait the due date of the martyrs' announcement", he says.

"After all, the enemy soldiers, have killed my son with his wife".

Grandma, tactically tries to divert the conversation. "To go on and on",... "with this irritating awful reality of the war",... "won't let us do our normal life", she says, mildly smiling.

"I feel you, there's nothing funny about it",... "I guess, it's good to share our old experience",... our life under the Italian colony".

"Enough all day long to talk about the weird war life", she says, her voice strained.

"I would prefer, not to recall the past, with the present", he advises his wife. He gets serious so quickly.

"Old age and dogs, they come, without being called", he says, looking at her, to gauge her reaction to his say.

"To your wise words, I agree one hundred percent",... "but still we're lucky, we're breathing",... She sighs, "Bad wind of suffering, blowing around our grand-children life.

"We hated our Italian colonizers as they said "Eat and don't speak".... "What will you say, for our own brothers our liberators of the land", when they, say "Don't eat and don't speak"?

The village is almost empty. One, can see, only old people, walking here and there. You don't see, youth's of young generation. They either left the country or joined the armed resistance.

"I'm really worried", Anna says, as she approaches the demolished house of her parents. Voiceless, stands still, looking down to the ground, her eyes blinking, tears coming out down her cheeks. Asli, steps towards her, alarmed by her situation. "The bloody assassin enemy, have destroyed my only house, my parents possess" Anna says.... "I didn't escape, from what I feared" she adds.

"Don't get into trouble", Asli says.

"I can't pretend my griefs either",... "I can't stand it anymore", Anna responds.

"I know", pauses for seconds,... "But you have been, through this, since the time, you joined the resistance" Asli responds, not disregarding the truth of her view.

"This time I take it personally",... "it'll be the worst day, I'll ever remember in my life, She says, looking at her, eyebrows raised.

Asli, gets a little nervous, "Have courage", my dear,... "I hope all your family are safe", she says, patting her back.

They proceed walking, to a nearby house. It's Anna's Grandparent house. "I'm getting nervous", Anna says, breathing out deep. "That house you see",... "it's of my Grandparents, she adds, pointing towards the house. "I can't believe that",... "the whole village is quiet",,,, "no people are there" she repeats, scared and muttered.

Where am I going exactly?

Grandma's out in the sun, alone on her own, sitting on a stool. Suddenly, she sees from a near distant, both Anna and Asli, stepping towards her. Wonders, for seconds, while trying to look at them, using her tiny eyes.

Anna, steps close to her Grandma. Asli, stomps out as she follows, Anna's footstep.

"Grandma! Grandma!" she shouts.

"Who are you?" She says, struggling, to raise up from her seat.

"I'm Anna! Anna",... "your Grand daughter", says in a loud voice, stepping, close near to her ear. A dream like, a fantasy begins to swirl around in her mind.

"Anna! Anna!" She repeats, trying to shout, a shout of joy.

A sound of "Elilta!" Dominates the area, to the point of waking up the neighborhood. Anna grabs her hands, closely leaning towards her, she embraces, hugs and kisses Grandma, for quite time.

"Where's Grandpa?"... "Is he fine?" Anna asks. Closes her eyes for seconds.

"He's fine" responds.

Grandma, leads her towards the house. Grandpa, is still on his bed, half sleep. There's something sitting in his mind, that kept him from thinking, about what's really tearing him up inside. He's searching his head.

Anna steps towards her Grandpa's bed in a tip-toe.

"Everything is fine with you Grandpa?" She asks, glancing with a smile at his face.

He "nods", trying to smile.... "I'm fine, despite my old age", he adds.

"Glad to here that" Anna says.

Grandma, steps towards her and grabs her hand, inviting her to the kitchen. "Let me make some tea", Grandma says, to avoid a further discussion, with Grandpa, about the reality of the whole family. Hands her a cup of tea. Anna, makes her first sip.

"Nice tea!"... "How're you feeling Grandma?" She asks.

"Well",... "as our wise fathers say",... "Don't ask anyone how one is but see his/her face",... "I myself can't complain, she responds.

"So how do you see me?" Grand daughter, She asks. "Very good!"... "Despite the years waging on you".

Asli, with the baby on her chest, steps towards the kitchen. "Who's she?" Asks Grandma.

"My comrade", responds Anna.

"What to mean by that?" Grandma asks.

"Sorry to use, the revolutionary word",... "I mean",... "She's one of the Freedom fighters. Grandma, looks at the baby.

"Who's baby it's?"

ASli, intervenes. "It's Anna's baby" she responds. Grandma, tries to smile at the Baby.

"Cute baby!

Anna and Asli keep quiet. Asli, hands the baby to Grandma.

"I'm so happy to see my Grand daughter with her baby", sighs. "The revolution took this long",... "though we're happy, with the independence.

"How old's the baby? Asks Grandma. "Only three days", responds Asli.

"Don't tell me, he's born the same day of the Independence Day?".

"It's she Grandma, a baby girl", says Anna. She laughs, "no difference at all", responds. "How Grandma?"

"The revolution, is equal share, of males and females".

Asli's home.

Asli's about to leave them, to go to her own family. Anna, accompanies her out. Both look at each other. Asli, leans against her ear,

"I'm glad to meet your Grand Parents",... "especially your Grandma's, in a good posture psychologically", says Asli.

"Me too", responds Anna. "I'm surprised, to see Grandma, eloquently communicating".

"See you soon", says Asli as she leaves her, walking down the street.

Anna, walks back stepping towards Grandma.

"I really, liked your com...com..." says Grandma, trying to come up with the new word correctly.

"Comrade!" Grandma, Anna responds.

"Well when is she coming back?" I hope soon.

Asli, on her way home she feels, happy. Her son Sami's taken care, under Martyrs kids orphanage, then in a place called Ararb, and now after the Independence, at St. Joseph school Keren.

Finally, she reaches her home. She looks up straight towards her family's house, twenty years, after her absence. Her mind buzzes with fear as she steps forward. Looks down, wondering, if she's ever to meet her parents alive. She sighs, thinking about, how life was hard, under the enemies hand. She sees a quick pain in her eyes. Approaches, the door, still her mind filled with doubt. Stands, right in front of the door, ready to knock. Shuts her eyes tight and begins to knock, lightly.

With sound of a knock, her Mother, rushes towards the door. Stands behind the door, for seconds, her mind refusing to open. Then, she decides to open it, her leg trembling.

Finally she opens the door. First, she stares at her, with fear, not knowing, she's her daughter.

"Mommy! Mommy!" Asli shouts.

Mom, opens the door widely, to let her in, getting shocked in surprise.

"Are you really Asli? She says, in her mind, two reality crashing. The reality of being a martyr and survivor of the war. Both stare at each other, as a mixed feeling, of joy and sorrow, clouds their minds.

Asli, jumps onto her mother, grabbing her hands, leaning so close to her chest, to give her a hug and a kiss.

"Come on in" Mom invites her, gripping her hands lightly. Asli, steps inside, still holding her Mom's hand. Both sit on an old sofa. Asli, rolls her eyes around, just to see, no changes on all the setting of the house. Mom, smiles at her, realizing she's about to bring, the old remembrances.

"How're you mama? She asks.

"I guess alright", responds Mom, taking a deep breath. Asli, "nods" gazing at her, smiling.

"How do you feel my presence? Asli asks. The place get quiet for seconds. Suddenly, Mom squeals as Asli smile at her.

"I feel good, no doubt about it", she respond, smiling back at her.

"Where's my father?" Asli asks, feeling fearful. She sighs, thinking about how to give her an answer.

"I know how you miss your Daddy", she says, breathing lightly, in a low voice. Asli, stays quiet for seconds. Though, mentally not ready, to tell her, about her Daddy's whereabouts, after taking a quick glance at her.

"Unfortunately, your Daddy passed away, few months before the Independence" she says, crying and crying.

Asli, joins her Mom crying.

"I won't meet him again",... "Things would be clicking alone",..." Very sad not to see him alive, she murmurs in grief.

"I miss all his kindness",..." I just miss him", she shouts, in despair mood. Mom, keeps silent, following, the cultural tactic, of let it go, without saying anything.

Death announcement day.

In the absence of Anna, Grandma and Grandpa discuss on how to inform, about the death of her parents.

"I'm kind worried on how to tell, Anna", Grandma voices. "I have an idea", Grandpa says.

"What's your idea? She asks.

"Just give her, a wise and temporary information". But "How?" She says.

By telling her, that her parents are in "Bahri", (a farming location, along the southern Red Sea coast). "Good idea, for now that'll work".

"We've got to call neighbors, before we tell her, I guess" he says.... "No one surprises, about bad news".... "To be up front and tell the situation, won't be good idea".

Late in the afternoon, the neighborhood, female and male Elders, gather at their house. "Merdii" (the death announcement), follows a cultural way. It should never be, a surprise like white people do.

In the middle, Grandma stands and says, "Now is the proper time, to tell Anna, the death of her parents".

An elder woman Mrs. Fana, is selected, to lead the process. She takes a deep breath, before she starts to speak. All eyes are on to her. Silently, stepping towards Anna, "Both of your Parents are dead", she says, in a whisper tone.

Anna, abruptly, jumps up from her seat and starts to cry loudly. Mrs. Fana again approaches her. "Be strong" she says. Grandma, tries, to wipe off her tears, running down her cheeks. "Unfortunately, that awful day of the massacre",... "about one hundred people were killed",... "among them being your parents", Grandma says. A low sound of a cry, tuned in melody, so smooth and well guided, dominates the house.

After an hour, to terminate the tuned melody of the cry, Mrs. Fana raises her voice and says, "Swallow it", swallow it.

All stop crying.

In a moment, when silence dominates the house, Anna enters into a deep thought. She begins to revisit, her experience of war and survival.

"This is the revolution, a sacrifice being particular in its kind".... "Death is a common denominator".... "As one joins, there's only a chance of survival, death, or getting injured".... "I wish I died, get martyred", she repeats in a formal reaction.

The grieving session, suddenly, changes its tone to another mood. All get chatting. Male elders peers, are sitting on one corner of the house, while females on the other, facing face to face, in a circle. The center of their chatting, is about the dead members, of the family. They mostly raise, the positive aspect, of their life.

Mr. Haile picks on his wife. He, says, "you remember the day I was over drunk?

His wife, Hellen interrupts his say. "You mean the day you pretended to be dead?

"You got it" he responds, wincing.

"I simply hide my breath",... "just to check on you", he says getting serious and not laughing.

"Check on you!" what do you mean, she says, smiling at his face.

"I did it on purpose, to see if you really loved me", he says, in the middle giggling.

All at the same time laugh.

Mr. Haile again turns his face to Anna.

"Do you",... "Freedom fighters, ever grieve?, Throws the question to Anna.

"Of course we do", she says, blinking at him for seconds. "Exactly, like our cultural version?" He asks again.

"Not exact, quite different version, responds, Anna responds.

"We would like hear from you about the different version",... "if possible in detail", he says, inviting her, to share her experience.

Grinning, with all she got, "Well" I'm ready to tell the other version" she says.

"All's, about how the revolution, have disciplined us"....

"No organized funeral".... "Buried where one fallen". "Awet N'Hafash", (Victory for the masses), follows, the last honoring farewell phrase.

Anna stops.

All around her, start talking, commenting, sometimes laughing at each other.

"Very, strange!" says Mrs. Manna, exerting one after the other nods, sitting at the corner near the door.

"You call yourselves Freedom fighters",... "by the way aren't you Christians? Mr. Haile, throws in a question.

"Yes, we're, but disciplined not to mention of it", she responds, surprising him in a blink.

"My mind can't digest it, to think of it",... "it's very horrible in kind", he says, scratching up his forehead.

Food and drinks is served. Most of the women, keep their attention on Anna.

"I'm curious if I may ask you a question", says Mrs. Manna, feeling so shy to open her mouth. Anna gives her a quick smile, "sure, what is your question?

"I would like to know, some other revolution disciplines, she asks, managing to collect her herself.

"I definitely will", she says, evidently irritated by the past of her experience, life under the armed resistance.

"You know, after any military operations, there was "Bahli", (a party accompanied, by revolutionary songs and cultural dance, organized, without any rehearsal).

All are silent.

To break their silence, Anna continues. "I guess, nothing seems important, to convince you to believe me",... "but that's the reality".... "I'll add something strange, hard to believe to all this.

"A tuned "Krar", (a six-string musical instrument), with all its melody, revives our spirit",... "just to distract the fighters, from the shocks and trauma, after war".

All get stunned, to all her say.

Mrs. Manna, voices in a low tone, sighing. "All in all of what you say",... "you celebrate the death",... "am I right?

"Right", she responds. "It's actually, about perception differences, that I was part of it, I guess".

"Sorry to interrupt you, "in our culture we celebrate, what to be celebrated",... "I mean, weddings, birth days, neighborhood festivity",... "but we culturally, mourn for death".

Late in the evening.

All neighborhood mourners leave the house. The house becomes quiet. Anna moves close to her Grand Parent, as they are sitting side by side. She's almost to forget, the tragic death of her Parents.

Leans, towards her Grandma right ear, in a whisper tone, like to tell her of something. "I don't see my two young brothers around here", where are they? She asks.

Grandma, gets perplexed on how to give her an answer. Backs her head backward. "I don't want to afflict you with another bad news again", she responds.

"Bad news?", she asks.

"I wonder how your mind takes it",... "but your two young brothers, have dis-appeared from the neighborhood".

"Where?" she says, remaining un movable and speechless.

Grandpa, gets up from his chair and intervenes, looking at Anna in a moment.

He sighs, hoping to calm the situation.

"Well" to make the story short, your two young brothers, are still safe and alive, he says, looking down to cool her embarrassment.

"So where are they?" asks Anna, crossing her arms. Tears won't come out.

"Your two brothers are living, with an old Widow, about 14 km, away from our village", Grandpa responds.

"Damn the revolution!" Anna pronounce loudly. "Don't get mad." Grandpa responds.

Grandma joins their conversation. She stands before Anna, something flickering across her face.

"Something bad?" Grandma says, who heard Anna cursing the revolution.

"I am sorry for that, Grandma, Anna says apologizing. Grandma says nothing.

Two days later.

Anna, travels on foot, heading towards the village. As she approaches the village, sees many children, playing local games, on an empty green field.

All dressed in a military, Anna, walks silently, around the field, pretending to watch the game. By chance, one of the kids, runs towards her, leaving the field. At first, he gets little shy and looks down, not to see her face.

"Hey" she says, in a low tone, not to scare him, because of her military vestment. He looks back at her suspiciously.

"Do you know" mentioning the name of her two brothers, playing on the field? She forwards, clearing her throat.

"I'm one" he says.

"What's your name? She adds.

"Mehari" he says again looking at her face. "Oh, is your brother with you playing?" "Yes", he says, pointing out to his brother.

He calls from far his brother to come to him. His brother, in rush runs towards them.

Anna, hadn't seen her family, in twenty years, since she joined, the armed resistance. Caught up, in her own story, as a Freedom fighter, she stays silent, not to reveal her identity.

"Who is she?" asks the brother, looking side way to Anna.

"No need to guess, she's for sure, one of the fighters, answers Mehari.

"At least you should have asked her name? Am I right?"

"You're right, but she didn't want to tell her name, responds Mehari.

As there's nothing left to say, Anna, steps few yards away from them. Again repeating himself, did she tell you, of who she's? Asks his brother.

"No" responds Mehari,... "please don't bother me with dumb questions.... "I've no time to respond you".

Anna, steps towards them, and stops still, glancing back at them, as she sees the shock on their faces.

"You think maybe, we ought to find a place, where to go?" She asks, looking at their eyes. They both get silent, then shake their heads.

"Where to go?" She asks again.

"Just follow us, you can stay with us, at the house of the old Lady", Mehari responds.

"Thank you for the chance", she adds.

Both lead her, walking down a twisted path, towards the small "Hidmo", (a rectangular house made of giant woods, straws and clay). Finally, they're to reach near the house.

The old Lady, is outside, enjoying the morning sun, reciting her prayers. Her tiny eyes, immediately focus, to see from a near distant, both brothers with the stranger, walking towards the house. The Old Lady, invites all to get in, in the little "Hidmo". Mehari, steps, towards the traditional oven, made of clay, to prepare some tea. His brother, is silently sitting between Anna and the Old Lady. Anna restricted her mind, not to reveal her identity, for a moment. She, already knows about the situation, but she's playing smart.

"Tea is ready" says Mehari, pouring the tea into plastic cups. All enjoy drinking tea. Suddenly, the Old Lady, stands from her seat, in a low tone, she orders to prepare the woods, mentioning the name "Hidru". He steps outside with Mehari, his brother to give him hand.

Anna and the Old Lady, remain chatting inside the house. Half of the puzzle is solved, as Anna hears the name Hidru.

"These two kids are of your own?"... "Maybe, your grandsons?" Anna asks, though she's confident, that's not true.

"No, actually they're not mine, but God given kids"....

"They're orphans".... "Father and motherless", she adds.

"Sorry for that",... "but how have you, happened to take care of them?" Anna asks.

"The day, I first saw them, rambling on the street, I collected them to live with me", responds the Old Lady....

"I'm lucky, to have them live with me", she adds.

"You did a good job", Anna responds, though she observes, poverty is dancing in the house. Anna glances at her with a sweet smile.

"Anything, I can help? Asks the Old Lady.

Anna, studies her kind gesture for few moments. "I've something to tell you", she says.

"What?", the Old Lady, gasps.

Both remain quiet, as Anna is struggling on how to tell her.

Anna, tries to be serious at the same time feeling pity, to express herself in a plain language. Tears run down her cheeks. She cries and cries in front of the Old Lady. Looks one time, over at her.

"The two of your kids, that you're taking care, are my brothers", she says.

"Are you kidding me? Replies the Old Lady, she too weeping, looking stunned.

Anna, leads her out, stepping towards her brothers. In a loud voice she calls both, by their names.

"How did she know about my name? Asks Hidru, excited and more confused.... "Did you tell her, my name, by the way?"

No, I didn't, replies Mehari.

Both run towards her. Anna, turns her head towards the Old Lady, feeling a dual feeling.

"It makes me happy to meet my brothers",... "at the same time make me sad", she says, to the Old Lady.

"I'm so glad, finally you found your brothers",... "never get sad", says the Old Lady.

Approaches, both of them, as they are standing in front of the door.

"I'm Anna your older sister", she says, in a low voice. Both glance at each other, freezing where they stand.

"Anna!" Anna! Both shout at the same time, jumping in joy. "How can this happening? Says Hidru.

Both kneel down, at the foot of the Old Lady, kissing her feet, again and again.

The Old Lady concludes the scene, by giving them, her blessing and all depart.

PART ONE

Etio-Eritrea war.

Anna is in her mid forty. Eight years after being discharged from the military, in 1998 a war broke between Eritrea and Ethiopia. The whole world, is occupied, with soccer game, taking place in France and the supper power USA, is in the middle of Impeachment, of its own President Clinton.

This time, the town of Badme, became the main issue of the conflict, between the two rivals. A tiny town on the border, became famous at least in the international news outlets.

From both sides, tactically, supporters emerged, equally cheering like its soccer game, without any political foundations.

Anna, is recalled to join the army.

That day, she rushes towards Down-town. Down-town, is full of folks, civilian mingled with X-fighters are rambling on the main streets. The local TV and Radio are broadcasting, about the war engagement, in defusing the danger of the war.

Anna meets, with several X-fighter, of her own unit. To her surprise, Asli is together with the group.

"Asli, Asli" shouts, Anna stepping towards her, her face being pale, because of the new war situation. Both retreat, to a small Tea-shop, to be on their own, sitting face to face.

Anna presses down her head, cursing. Asli, looks around and kicks the floor harder with her feet.

"We are freaked out, like a little kid", Asli says, hitting her knees with her hand repeatedly.

"Back to square one", Asli says, trying to hide her fear, squeezing her fingers. "Any idea of how this new war started", Anna asks.

"It's a weird surprise",..."No clue", Asli responds.

"I don't understand about this new war", Anna says, sipping hot tea.

"Me neither" responds Asli, as she tries, to take a sip.

"We have in common a crazy regime",... "nothing to do about that, Anna says, her hate of the previous war bombarding her mind.

Two other X-fighters join their conversations, all sitting, across a round table. Alem, sees them in a bad mood.

"This war isn't our war, at all", he says, his voice turning low. "The situation is dragging us",... "to a level of disregarding, the previous war, for the independence", adds Alem, looking at Anna and Asli.

"That'll be our own war",... "but I doubt, about this one", says Asli.

"Something is wrong with this war",... "someone has to take responsibility", says Andom, with a newspaper in his hand, looking back to read the articles of war.

The newspaper front pages reads, "War for our sovereignty".

"What a hell, they're talking about?" Andom sighs, leaning forward showing them, the newspaper article.

Anna, breaths deep.

"Our life, is hardly worth living, under such conditions of war, she sighs again.

"Already our joy of independence are fleeting", says Asli, pressing her lips together.

"Still, I've no desire to join the military", says Anna, shutting her eyes tight.

It seemed particular odd, for all the X-fighter, to join the military, without any convincing aim, to fight. The one that caused the war is the dual insistence, of the two regimes.

Under a banner of think our thought, the local people became, victims of the unexpected war.

At the military center.

After they have been discussing enough, about the war issue, all leave the Tea-shop, walking to the military, recruiting center. They make a long line, waiting their names to be called. Through a loudspeaker, Anna hears, her name been called, a couple of times. Anna, steps down the corridor, shifting her speed from slow to fast, just to be on time.

Walks in to the office, as the door is wide open.

The Army officer, sitting on his chair, greets her with a revolutionary greeting. The Officer smiles at her, inviting her to sit across on a chair.

"What's your name comrade" he asks, staring at her. "Anna", she responds, breathing a breath of let's go. Pulls out her file.

"Your nickname pleas?"

"My nickname!" She giggles.

He smiles, "Don't make me impatient". Again, "Your nick name! He asks.

Looks at him for a long moment, "you mean the one I got it, when I joined the revolution?

"Yes please!" He says.

"That name, it really sucks",... "I don't want, to be called, by that name anymore". "How will I know if you're an X-",...

Interrupts him in the middle, by saying, "X-Freedom fighter?" He turns serious. "Don't waist my time", he says, narrowing his eyes. Anna, keeps her eyes down.

Few seconds later, fixedly glances at his face. "Okay",... "I don't want to go to any argument", she says.

"I used to be called "Mortar", she says, showing her disguise, of the nickname.

"That would be all? She adds.

"Don't put me in trouble, I'm just doing my job", he says after a pause.

"It doesn't matter",... "the war that our regime devised",... "it's behind everyone",... "I just won't think of it". Pauses for another seconds.

"I fear the demand of our martyrs, is not fulfilled", she adds, raising her eyebrows, at her tone.

"Excuse me!"...

"I'm not entitled, right now, to deal with all, old and new",... "of your frustrations", responds, raising the files up his chest.

Again, he rests the files down on to the desk.

"After all these eight years",... "somehow peace, to hear about another war",... "for me is unacceptable.

He shrugs, "I probably have to stop, dealing with your feelings", he says, taking a deep breath.

"Back to the business", he says.

"By the way, do you know, the Female X-fighter, named by the name "Fenji"?

"I know her", replies, for his unexpected question. "How?"... "Are you related?" He asks, curiously.

"We...in the same...regiment", but why you ask me, about her?

"Just been exited for my own reason",... "a while ago, she was giving me hard time, the same as you".

Anna, steps out from the office, walking fast towards the exit door. Suddenly, she meets, Yasin, a veteran, disabled X-

Freedom fighter, at the threshold. "Are you here, for the same dumb military recall?" Asks, looking a little warier.

"Yes I'm" responds.

"I wonder, they wouldn't mind, even to dig, the martyrs grave",... "to recruit them back again",... "for this none sense war", she says, staying quiet for a while.

"Oh, the war saga, wouldn't leave us in peace", Yasin responds, standing speechless, staggering left and right, with his artificial leg.

Weird time.

Grandpa and Grandma, are together at home, just waiting for Anna, to come back.

"This was the free Eritrea, everybody was expecting? Forwards in a question, glancing at Grandpa.

"The rumor of another war, is circulating around, just to ruin our normal life", he says, his mind bombarded by, the thirty years of war, for the independence.

In years, a built-up, false praise, of the Dictator Isayas Afewerki, made him confident and be in power for so long. Though, practically, he pretended not to accept the praise, his own picture of himself, is still on the peoples mind.

"The destructive wish",... "just to ruin the whole Society, is ridiculous", says Grandpa, scratching his head hardly.

"What's the difference, between the Dictator. Isayas and the Emperor, Haile Silasie?" She asks, in an open question, that came to her mind.

"Both are un elected, for sure",... "idolized by their own people",... "to the point of being worshiped", he says, clenching his teeth.

This is it.

Anna, on her way home, totally feeling sad and upset, walks down a dirty path, towards her village. Before she is to reach home, sits on big rock under a big tree. Her mind moving swiftly, enters into a kind of day dream vision, talking to herself.

"I doubt, if this is the dream of our martyrs", she says, moving her lips up and down. Instantly, connects her mind, with her martyr husband. She mentally, parks where she is, sitting speechless. One after the other, without interrupting her thought, the voice from above, bombards her mind. She remains cool, calm and collected. The voice instructs her, about things that she's aware of.

"Believe me", the voice say, "we know who we are, as freedom fighters". "The aim of the revolution, that was tactically hidden, from our eyes",... "our innocent civilian people are paying for it". The voice, then vanishes.

Anna, proceeds walking down the path. Her daughter, is playing outside, with a couple of her peers. She only minds, about the game, she is playing with her peers, until she sees her mother standing behind her.

"Mom, I didn't expect you, it's nice and cool out", Saba says, smiling wide.

Picks a banana, from her bag and hands her.

"Go ahead playing", she says, patting her back and grins. "I'll see you in a moment Mom", Saba says, feeling joyful.

Saba, shares the banana with her peers. Instantly, Anna looks back and observes her daughter, sharing the banana.

"Good job", she says, remembering the good time, she passed during the resistance.

By the time she gets home, she sees both of her Grandparents, sitting side by side, seemingly not talking to each other. All their attention is, on the current affair of war, listening it, from their small battery Radio, all day long.

Anna steps in.

"Are you alright!" She says.

""How have you been?" She greets them, as she feels pity for their loneliness.

"Nothing to complain!"... "We're good", responses Grandma, to her greetings.

An awkward pause follows. Sits besides them. A dead sort of silence, fills the house. Anna feels more uncomfortable, to tell them about the new unexpected plan.

"I hope you're following the news affairs", she says.

"Yes, we're" responds, Grandpa moving his radio towards him.

"We're in the middle of war",… "unfortunately I'm recalled, to join the army", she says, blinking her eyes.

"Never thought, we would hear about that", Grandpa voices, feeling down morally.

"I've only twenty-four hours, to leave the house",… "so let me organize packing", she says.

Grandma's eyes dart towards Anna.

"A house built in a hurry, crumbles early", she whispers.

"This time the situation turned around me", says, holding her breath.

There's a long pause.

"Lord have mercy" Grandpa voices.

"Right now my heart is pounding",... "I've no idea of what to do next", she says, getting quiet for a moment. She's deeply sad, about her daughter, on how to tell her. The only thing, she's proud of, is her daughter.

Early in the morning, before the Sun is to rise, gets up from her bed. She walks right and left in tip-toe, not to wake up her daughter. Suddenly, Saba half-asleep, her eyes half open, "Mommy! Mommy", shouts.

Anna takes a breath, looks around, "Sleep!" "Sleep!" baby,... "it's early for you, to be up and straight", she says, in a sweet voice, rubbing her head.

Moment later, she falls, into a deep sleep again.

Anna walks out. Grandparents follow her footsteps. She walks back, to give them a kiss and hug.

"Did you tell your daughter, about you leaving?" Grandma, asks, stepping one step backward.

"No I didn't", she responds.

"You don't think, it's crazy idea, not to tell her, by yourself?" Grandma asks.

Anna shrugs, "I do",... "but I didn't want, she, to be on my way.

Anna, on her shoulder, with all her stuff, packed in back-bag, departs walking down the main street. Stands along the street, under a tree, looking left and right, waiting for any passing by, vehicle. Suddenly, she sees a military Jeep running on the street. Raises her hands up. The Jeep stops.

The driver, lowers the side window glass and in high tone, invites her to move towards them, stepping fast.

"I guess you are heading towards the Capital", the Driver asks, not knowing her identity, whether to be a civilian or X-fighter. Gets in through the back door. A Major who is sitting besides the Driver, looks back. She leans close to the window, trying to lower the window.

"Your look, looks like you're an X-fighter, am I right?" Says the Major, glancing at her side way.

Wrinkles her face as mean as she can.

"By the way, how did you figured out",... "I'm an X-fighter?" She asks.

"The way you walk", he giggles. She laughs.

"To mean what?" She says.

"Your steps look, like a military steps.

"Whatever you say, is not a surprise, but your guess is right, I guess", she says, looking up to the ceiling of the car.

After Anna left, Grandpa and Grandma, retreat to their house, stepping in a slow motion.

Saba, is still on her bed, sleeping, turning her body, right and left. Not to wake her up, for the moment both keep quiet, for the fear of not to be asked, of her Mom's whereabouts.

A few minutes later, wakes up from her sleep, still staying at her bed, moving her eyes up and down, left and right.

"Mom", Mom she voices, while still on bed. Grandma steps towards her bed.

"Now we are in trouble", she says, speaking to herself. Grandma stays tense, keeping her eyes on to her.

"Mom's out for the moment", she says, dabbing her upper body, over the blanket.

"Breakfast is ready", voices Grandma, an honest fear resting on her face. Both smile at each other. "I usually, don't take my breakfast, till later, any way, Saba says, as she stops looking at her.

"Where's my Mom?"... "I don't see her around", she asks, to Grandma.

Grandma, tries her best, not to show her worry. Suddenly, the name of Anna's friend Asli, interjects her mind.

"Your Mom left, for a short visit, to Asli's village", she says. "She's coming back in two weeks time", she adds, to calm her down.

There we are.

The war already started a week ago. All military movements are in the dark. Dozens military trucks, are ready, parked alongside the main road. Anna, walks all the way, up to the trucks. Few minutes later, she sees Asli, walking down the street. Anna, voices in a loud tone calling her name. Asli in a hurry steps towards Anna. Both hug and embrace, kissing each other. Asli steps one step backward, her eyes still fixed to Anna.

"Again, we're in this together? Says Asli, in her mind remembering the old days.

"The old ugly thing, of war is following us",… "but at least we're lucky to be together", responds Anna.

A Military man, standing, in the middle of the parked trucks, three times blows his whistle. With a megaphone on his hand, loudly recites the order, to all who are standing and waiting to be loaded.

"Everyone on board" he shouts, as all try, to get on the back of the trucks. Both Anna and Asli ride at the back, sitting together on the floor.

"It's a pity, to go on fighting, without some assurance, says Anna, her voice trailing. Both, exchange glances.

"It's the regime, the one that'll all get us killed", Asli responds.

"They're not either concerned with our life", Anna says, staring down the floor. "I wonder if ever we survive this war", she says, in a low voice, leaning near her ear.

"All, we're victims, not of our choice", Asli says, all her body shaking.

"By the way, did you inform your daughter, about you leaving?" Asli asks, gazing at her, not smiling.

Anna, moves her head down.

"No, I didn't", she says, not feeling, to start to recite the story, again.

"I feel you, how horrible, it's", responds embarrassed. Finally, they reach their destination.

Anna, is staged with the heavy Armored division 16, as a radio operator, forty km, away from the border. While.

Asli is ordered to join the ground force, as radio operator, at the border trenches.

The war becomes so tense, this time different in its intensity. Wave after wave, the enemy soldiers, fight, a close distance battles. Short range bombs, begin to rain, all over the trenches, ramming here and there.

A Colonel as he observes the fierce fight, heated up, he steps towards Anna, who is kneeling on the ground, with her radio transmitter on the ground. From behind, leans towards her.

"Any ground advance, you are informed about?" He asks, calling her by her nick name.

"Not yet", she answers", being deeply pressured by the sound of the bombs. He clears his throat.

Suddenly, her radio crackle several times. Asli is on the other end.

"The enemy over run our trenches", says Asli in a high tone. "That's awkward", Anna responds.

Turns the radio on a speaker, to allow the Colonel listen. Short range bombs, started to fly all over the aria. The fighting approaches near to them, so close to hear the bullet sound. Tension bounces between them. After a minute of pause, Anna dials. Asli, immediately picks the phone. While still communicating, a bomb falls several yards from Anna, exploding. She falls to the ground, her radio transmitter still on her hand. She gravely is injured her leg, trying to bandage it with her cloth. Instantly she faints, lying on the ground. Her radio is still on.

On the other end, Asli, repeatedly calls Anna. Anna, is struggling to stop the bleeding. She interrupts communicating with Asli, when Asli voice is still heard.

"Hello" Hello, no answer. "Hello" Hello, no answer again. The Colonel, picks the radio.

"Anna, Anna" she shouts on his ear.

"It's the Colonel", responds in a calm voice.

"Things are not going to our plan",... "so my order is an immediate retreat from the Eastern trenches"... "and move to south".

"Its ugly situation, but I'll communicate your order, to our front line leader", Asli responds.

Four male freedom fighters, with a stretcher, rush towards Anna. Lay her on the stretcher and walk towards the first aid center. Anna, is lightly groaning. All try to console her, as she is breathing too hard.

"Are you afraid of dying?" Asks, one of the freedom fighter. "No", she says, "I'm just not ready", she adds.

Why? He asks.

She sighs, "this time I don't want to die, for one reason only",... "I don't want my baby, to be orphan of a mother.

A few minutes later, they reach the center. A Male and Female field Nurses, get ready to assist Anna. The Female Nurse asks.

"How long she has been bleeding", she asks, looking side way, to an X-fighter.

"I guess between ten and fifteen minutes".

Anna looks to her wounded leg and starts crying.

"It's alright, you gone be fine", Female Nurse says, sounding real confident.

Saba's heart banged.

Almost a week passed, since Saba, don't see and hear about her Mom's whereabouts.

"Are you holding secret about my Mom?" Saba says, looking down, warily.

"Come on and sit with me", says Grandma, just to distract her, from further questioning.

"Get to hoping, your mom is going to come soon", she adds. She goes on crying.

"Stop crying", voices Grandma.

"I don't have any good things left", Saba says, in whisper tone talking to herself.

For a minute, she wonders.

"Why things are the way they are?" She asks, herself to her self, contemplating about the absence of her Mom.

Grandpa, joins their conversation.

"I feel bad, about all Anna's actions",... "just leave us, in a worse situation", he says.

"I don't know what to do with Saba".... "Now and then she's insisting, about whereabouts of her Mom" she says, impatiently.

Pulls back, from her Grandma and goes out to play with her peers.

"Damn",... "it feels good out here", "I just...I can't stay home for so long, to see only my Grandparents", she says.

A female peer her name Mimi, in a whisper tone, leans against her ear.

"What about your Mom, isn't she there?" She asks. Saba gets silent. Mimi, holds her two hands tighter. Saba, starts to cry, tears coming out down her cheeks. Mimi, "Saba!"... "Saba!" shouts in a low voice and kisses her forehead softly. Mimi, makes her sit up and drink water.

"You know", Saba says, straight forward to tell the truth. "Know what?" Mimi asks.

"My Mom is an x-freedom fighter". She mutters. "After being discharged from the military, she's recalled to fight the new war." Saba adds.

The others peers who are playing local games invite Saba to join them playing. Saba, resists to join them and walks towards home.

Amputation.

Anna, is transferred to a big hospital, in the capital, to get further treatment. Doctors, Nurses and other Hospital workers, wearing their proper white and colored gowns, are moving here and there. The Hospital is crowded with many other wounded fighter.

Anna, looks exhausted, from the bad wound, she got only one month ago. She remains, lying on the bed, groaning lightly, as two Nurses accompanied by a Doctor, step towards her bed. Suddenly, she slightly opens her eyes, just to see, surrounded, seemingly, by strangers. One more time, looks up and sees, by who she's been surrounded. Draws her hands up to her face, as if she's shielding herself, from some kind of attack. The doctor, offers her a quick smile and greets her.

"How're you?.

She tries to face him, but her pain is so high, no strength, to respond to his greetings. Without saying any word, "nods" breathing too hard.

The Doctor and a Nurse walk out, while one Nurse remain in the room. The Nurse, holds her hands over the age, just to test her temperature. Hands her, the temperature kit glass, to insert it into her mouth. Checks her heart beat. Installs the infusion stand, straight beside her bed. Keeps her eyes, on the infusion bag, to set it to the standard flow, of the drips. After inserting and connecting the plastic tubes, looks at her watch and leaves the room, without saying anything.

Few hours later, the Doctor and the two Nurses meet at his office, to converse about Anna's situation.

"All in all, her situation is not good",... "unfortunately our medical consensus, is to amputate her leg", The Doctor says, he sighs.

"I feel sorry for her", one of the nurse, responds, admitting the situation, how hard it'll be.

All agree to the doctor's order for the amputation. The amputation date is set with the consent of Anna.

In a status of preoccupations.

It's almost three months, since Anna left the house to join the military. Grandma, gets very worried, about the ongoing war. Being alone on her own, enters in to a deep thought.

She's pushed to enter into a status of preoccupation, that her mind can't handle. Her mind started, to travel back and forth. Too many questions come to her mind.

Grandpa after getting enough suns heat, he steps towards the house. He sneaks a look up at her, just to distract her, from what's going on, in her mind, offering her a good smile. She sits still as a stone, staring at him.

"Your mind is still grinding",... "the old story, I guess", he says.

Her mouth fall open to respond.

"In this cursed country, the old and the new are mixed", she says. "Before we were to heal from the old wounds",... "here the new comes, right in our eyes", she murmurs.

"I feel you", he says,... "From that one this one is worse" he adds.

"I hate these revolution stuff, they better give us a break", she says, looking shocked. Closes her eyes, fighting her frustrations.

In the middle of their conversation, they see Saba, stepping towards the house. Saba her head down, she hurries along the street. Her last conversation with her peers, is still racing on her mind.

"I wish my Mom was a simple civilian" she says, prioritizing, against the life of Freedom fighters. "By day for me",... "this's the hardest part",... "now and then",... "to insist, to ask my Grandparents, about my Mom", she says, talking to herself.

Steps inside the house. Both stop conversing and stay where they are sitting. Saba, sits besides her Grandma. Touches her arm. All are silent.

"I think you're more worried about all my asking". "Am I right?" She says, glancing with a smile, at her Grandma.

"Something one don't know, one wouldn't tell either", Grandma explains. Pauses for seconds.

"Let me tell you something", she says, in a whisper tone. "I guess it's about my Moms where about, am I right, asks.

"You know we're in the middle of war...so...so, your Mom have joined the military".

"It's bad news",... "I wish I was told earlier, she says. "I understand why you were holding, back to keep it secret, somehow",... "now I feel better", Saba says, swallowing it regardless.

I hope she's not dead.

Asli, stares at her signal radio, lied on the ground, three feet away, from her, sitting on the ground, under a small tree. No communication with Anna, since the day of the incident. A terrible quiet looms over her. The sureness in her eyes, drastically changes, one hundred eighty degrees.

"Maybe she is dead", she says, to herself. A little while, she sees, her line leader, stepping towards her. He stands over her, raising his eye-brows at her. She is sitting there in a daze, unable to speak.

"What's bothering you" he asks, rolling his eyes.

"I don't know if...", gets silent for seconds...." My buddy"... Tries to think of the incident, "is still alive".

"By the way, what's your buddy's name.

"I doubt you know her by her name",... "but I can tell you her nickname", she says and sighs.

"What's her nickname"? He asks. "Mortar".

He pulls back few steps smoking a cigar.

"She's just okay". He replies. Her impatience holds her down her smirk. "What really happened to her?" She asks.

"She's been injured her leg, got amputated and is on a recovery status".

"Is she alive?" Asli asks.

"I'm assuming, she's still alive".

The war somehow it lasted for two years. Militarily, the operations were classified into three big stages. The first, second and third round. Anna's injured in the first stage.

Before it turned to be a conventional war, somehow the International community, tried just to denounce and politically condemn. The first mediation staff, through the help of Ruanda-America, popped up on the news outlet. Though in itself was not one hundred percent satisfying, it would have been more effective, if the Eritrean regime have accepted it.

Various agenda of war were shuttling, between the minds, of the two leaderships. Somehow, for quite long time, it has disrupted, the attention of the mediators.

One time it became, a border issue, another time a security issue. The cause of the war, though could be varied, mistakes and miscalculations could be accepted. One thing, that's unacceptable, is to proceed with their war agenda. They knew was not the right thing. A U-turn, would be a wise decision, instead of proceeding, in vain, by contriving, intrigue after intrigue.

PART TWO

It just happened.

Great exasperated sigh follows. Here the mysterious number flushing in my mind. "44" is the number. In my cultures view point, it's a bud luck number. The number of "Ganen" (the Devil).

For years, it repeatedly was coming, now to my mind, appearing physically in my eyes. To conclude it's a kind of hallucination, I never had, the bad practice, of taking drugs. On January 20, 2009, the number flushed into my cell- phone. It was the Inauguration day, the day Barack Obama was to swear as the 44th president of America.

The immigrants from Eritrea, whom I was in touch with, they always had a story to tell. The story in its weird and negative sense. I revised the core problem, of why they desert to the affluent societies. It's not about money, neither to earn a good life. It's all about the endless war situation and the religious persecution, they face. Most of them they sing the same song, unfortunately, tuning to the war and the religious persecution. Murder, tragedy, imprisonment, uprooting the people, due to their political and religious views, the main case of their escape.

Where else to go.

Saba, now, that she is eighteen years old, she is forced to join the military. She's inside, cooking and doing chores of the day. Anna, is sitting on a chair, just silent and moving her eyes left and right.

"I'm scared but I can't help it out", Saba says, in low voice, rolling her eyes, for seconds.

"Why scared?" Mom responds, shaking her head, trying to stand up, with the help of her canes.

"I'm scared, about this weird military recruitments", she says, looking up and wrinkling her nose, at her. "Did you hear, anything, I'm not aware off", Mom asks.

"No nothing, but-...she stepping back to the kitchen. "But what?" She asks, wanting to know about the situation.

"I guess, I'm in the military conscript age", she says, pulling her hair down.

In bright day light, two military men show up, at the residence, wearing like civilians. They hardly bang at the door. Anna, mutters and heads straight for the door, stepping slowly, with her canes on her armpit. She opens the door halfway. At first she didn't suspect them to be military, because of their civilian ware. One of the military, moves closer.

"We're here to deliver this letter to your daughter".

Picks out from his pocket, a sealed envelop and hands to Anna. Anna slams back the door on their face and steps in. Saba, remains anxious, for minutes lingering in fear. Starts to dread, sitting quietly, her heart aching.

Anna, hands her the sealed envelop. She reckons, to open it and read it loudly.

"Who gave you? She asks, raising up and down the letter.

"I don't know, their identity, but they look like civilians" she responds, clearing her throat.

Saba, gives a little shrug.

"What's happening?" right now, Anna asks. Saba reads the address.

"Mom, it's unfortunately, about the military recruit call", she says,... "I'm ordered, to show up, at the military recruiting center by today", she says, stepping back some feet.

Only two hours left, for her to show up, at the recruiting center. She's running here and there in the house, completely acting out of her mind.

"Saba!" "Saba!", in a cry tone, shouts Anna. Closes her eyes, feeling the sort of awe-fear, of the regimes, political and moral recklessness. "Here again" she says,... "It's real curse, to see my only baby, to be snatched from my hand"....

"Isn't enough all my sacrifice, till giving my leg, to remain permanently disabled".

Saba, leaves her, on her own, rushing through the door, leaving the door half-open. Anna follows her, stepping slowly towards the open door. Saba is out of her sight, as she attempts, to see out there. Closes the door and walks back into the house.

Grandma and Grandpa, not knowing of what's going on, they step in the house. Anna remains silent, despite hearing their greetings.

"I see in your face, you are no right today", Grandma voices, in a lower tone.

"How can I be right, when things are not right", Anna responds, shaking her head up and down.

"What happened"? She asks.

"Saba is called by the military" she says, ashamed by the awful deed.

"This's a horrible thing",... "don't they own heart", Grandma says, tears running down her cheeks.

Saba never returned, to see her family, to say goodbye. That very day, with thousands new recruits, loaded on trucks they lead their way, to Sawa, the training camp.

Sawa training camp.

A week, after the arrival, of the new military recruits, Saba is together with thousands trainees, out on the field, ready to be assigned her line group and regiment. She happened to be assigned with the group of Sami. Sami, holding the paper of the list names, together, with dozen of them, locates to an allotted place. All are under a medium tent, sitting on the ground, ready to follow the first basic security instructions.

Sami, stands in the middle of them, just to give them directions. He goes over, reading the direction.

"As you hear the first whistle, you wake up from sleep and in ten minutes time, you all be here".... "No breakfast is served, until later",... "we'll have it, after we finish our training".... "Movement from one place to another are restricted". "In case there's need, it'll be only with the permission".... "For security reason, there will be, a daily cookies code, to be exercised". He finishes. "Any question", he voices. All remain silent and nod.

"Okay then".... "It's time for the physical training"....

"ready? He whistles three times.

All go jogging around the field. After thirty minutes of jogging, Saba gets fatigue and tired, she feels very thirsty. Cuts off her jogging, and runs towards Sami, to drink some water.

"I'm sorry, my trainer", she whispers,... "I'm very thirsty", she says. Both their eyes hang together.

"You need to finish jogging", he says. "No one is allowed to drink water during the training" he adds.

"Please do me a favor, allow me to drink water", insists politely.... "I hope you won't let me down", she says, moving closer to him.

"It'll be stupid to let you do",... "but it's okay for now",... "never ever ask any favor, do you get me?"

"Yes sir", "she Nods", rubbing her sweat from her face.

Goes back to her tent, a bottle of water in her hands, looking like she might cry.

She sighs, leaning back on her chair. Pulls out her pen from her pocket and starts to write on a piece of paper, her first day experience at the camp. Despite the loud noise, inside the tent, she tries to concentrate on her writing. Writes, about life in the camp, the awful weather, her group and Sami her trainer. Folds the paper, inserts it in an envelope not sealed. She knows, that she's supposed, to deliver the open letter, to be read, by the line leader, just for a security reason.

Steps towards Sami's tent, sneaking, without been noticed by other trainees. Sami's busy boiling water, for his tea. She stays stand before the Tent, for seconds. Sami, lets her in, focusing his eye, on the boiling water. With the envelope in her hand, steps in. He turns around and gazes at her, smiling mildly.

"Anything I can help", he says, somewhat eyeing her suspiciously.

"Sorry to disturb you", she says, narrowing her eyes.

She gets tense, standing still before him. Takes out the open envelop and hands to Sami. "I think, I ought to give you, UN sealed envelop", she says, believing she's doing the right way. "Where's the letter headed for" he asks, just looking at her curiously.

"To my Mom", she responds.

"I'm glad, you came with UN sealed envelop" he says, not trying to read the content of the letter.

"Guess what?"... "you know the rule and regulation of the camp, he says again gazing at her face not smiling.

She, nods.

He opens his mouth to agree with her action.

Offers her a cup of tea. Saba, looks at the cup of tea and smiles. After staying for quite time, she walks back to her tent.

The next night.

Saba, all in her military vestments, walks down a narrow dirt path, carrying her gun; under a bright light of a full moon cycle.

After walking for quite time, she gets tired and rests, under a big tree shade. Pulling her little military rug, she stretches it, on the ground. As she lays down, she puts her gun, besides her, on the ground. After a couple of minutes, she falls into a deep sleep, and enters into the dream world.

Suddenly, she starts to recite, all her dreams, set in a flow of a series of scenes, when she was six years old, growing up with her mother and her step-father. The day of the HOYE-HOYE festival, in its colorful cultural and social ambient, gears in her mind, as she is to be, the first female kid, to light the fire, of the opening, of the festival. Turning her body, to the left side, lightly snoring, all the picture, of her first day, of her school day, comes one by one. The good time she enjoyed with YONI her childhood friend, the last days, of Yoni, playing with her, before he died of meningitis; the anguish of losing her best friend; Saint Ann's school, with all the nuns, taking care of her. Suddenly, turning her body to the right side, before she wakes up, from her sleep, a colony of monkey's, sprouting from the woods, surround the area, some climbing trees and some, playing on the ground.

Saba, waking up from her sleep, half awake, taking her gun, she starts to shoot out, aimlessly on the air.

Walks back down the hill, towards her base, all her mind distracted, her gun on her shoulder. She reaches near the training camp checkpoint. One of the night Guard, out of fear, raising up only his head, points his gun towards Saba. "Stop! Stop! Don't move from where you are" he shouts, loudly…. "If ever you do, I will shoot you down", again, he shouts.

Saba, right away stops, looking right and left, trembling with fear.

"I hope, he will not pull, the dumb trigger".… "I'm in danger!

The guard, using, the war secret codes, of communication, that are usually called, secret cookies, he communicates with Saba, as she's still standing, where she is and obeying.

"Say the cookies! The cookies of the day" he yells "Notime! No time!"… "I'll shoot you right away".

She completely forgot, about the cookies of the day. Motion less, stands where she is.

"I forgot, the cookies of the day". I am Saba, I am Saba" she shouts. "Please don't shoot! Don't shoot, she repeats.

Suddenly, Sami, shows up from behind. In a loud voice, instructs the Guard, not to take any action.

"Hold on! Hold on! Don't shoot".

The Guard, turns back his head, as he sees, his officer Sami, is behind him.

"Okay, Okay", the Guard says, in a low voice.... "But I am following your order commander".... "Anyone, with no cookies, of the day, has to be shot down".... "Isn't that your order? Am I right?

Sami taps his back gently.

"You're totally right",... "an order is an order",... "but I suspected the voice of the female, looks like, one of our new trainees". "Any way, you did a good job, following the rules and regulations of our military system".

Sami walks few yards forward towards Saba. First, he instructs her, to drop her gun, on the ground.

"Drop your gun! Drop your gun.

Saba obeys his order and drops her gun.

Confidently, walks towards her. He notices, she is one of his trainees.

"Who are you to be on our base, this time of the night?"...

"Don't you know the cookies of the day?"

Saba, steps few yards, towards him. Suddenly, she stops right in front of him.

"I'm Saba, I'm Saba",... "sorry for not remembering, the cookies of the day".... "I was totally distracted'.

Cools down his voice tone, trying to instruct her, with half a smile on her face.

"You know, the military tactic is, for the safety of everyone and anyone".... "God forbid!"... "If the Guard shoots you, who will take the responsibility?".... "The law is the law, don't do it again, my dear.

Both walk, towards the military training camp tents, silently not talking to each other. Suddenly, Saba senses, something falling down, out of her pocket. It is the photo of Yoni her childhood friend. Tries to collect it from the ground, kissing it, silently.

"Oh, my God! I miss you Yoni", she says, talking to herself, in a low voice. Again and again kisses it. "Yoni, Yoni, you are in a better place, in heaven",... "as for me, I am struggling, to live a weird life, of war and more of killings".

Suddenly, Sami turns his head facing towards Saba.

"What are you trying to do?"... "I am kind of suspicious and curious. Glances at his face in a mild smile.

"Nothing! Nothing", she says.

She's still with the issue, of her being, on her own, that night, struggling, in a nightmare dreams and fighting, with the monkeys.

"I am sorry, to get dragged, into this problem"
"Believeme, I won't do, that dumb shit again, to risk my life", she says. He looks at her, side way, with a smile.

"It's good, that you are aware, of all your mistakes", he says, not to be rude on her.

"Well, you know, there's nothing else, I can do",   "besides shooting, to the air",... "to save my life" responds, feeling the fact of her mistake.

"That's crazy anyway", he says, letting his breath go.

"I'm sorry, my dear trainer".... "I failed, the law and military order, by my negligence, compromising my life, to the danger of death", she sighs.

He observes her conversations, his heart begins to beat on his chest, like a war drum.

"Don't do it again", he says, his face getting serious.

"By the way, I have heard several shots, are you the one who was shooting, on the air?" he asks.

Fear pressing against her body, stares down onto the ground. "Nods".

All her actions giving him pause he chuckles.

"Shooting at an enemy you don't see!" he says, waiting her something to say. Saba, tries to arrange, her undone Afro hair, with her hands, sighs.

"You know, I was scared of the monkeys".... "In fear of them I started to shoot aimlessly, to the air". His eyes half closed, tries to make, the issue more serious.

"You're safe I guess, but you wasted the bullets, for nothing".... "You know, bullets cost money?"... "Am I fair with you, or speaking nonsense things?"

Struggling with my issue.

Sami, that night considers in his mind, the last chat he had with Saba. Holding in himself her words, before he's to go to bed, he sits on a chair. It's deep into the night, exhausted, but not yet ready to sleep, kicks off his boots and lays down, on a wooden bed.

After several hours of his sleep, dreaming a night dream, wakes up by singing birds. Sits up on his bed, resuming his position, his head on his belly and his eyes close.

"I need to come clean with my issue, of my affair with Saba"...." I can't wait."..."I've to do something."

His mind being instantly alert, wears all his military vestment and steps towards the door. He frowns. "It'll just be okay, if ever am able to convince her." Looks around the area, his widened. "This girl's really strange!"..."there's something different about her"...."I'm just connected to her".

He walks out to the training field. Stands straight and whistles three times. All the trainees, run towards the field. Saba being lined on the first line, gazes at Sami, without smiling. When all get ready, Sami whistles one time, smoothing his jacket. All move jogging. After several rounds of jogging, in the middle

Saba stumbles on the ground. Sami comes behind her and stretches his hand, to raise her up.

Saba groan softly. Sits down, still holding Sami's hand. "Really it sucks!"...." Not knowing about this dumb training, whatever", says in a shaky hand.

He turns on his heel, sitting down besides her. Stares at her face not smiling. She looks down, at her worn out boots.

"What distracted you to fall on the ground?"..." Maybe, it's me your trainer that distracted you?" says, giving her his most charming smile.

"Non of it", she responds, not feeling comfortable. "I fall down only because of dumb, torn apart and warned", she repeats.

Sami's smile deepens, counting on her minor preoccupa tions. "Sure, I can find you a pair of boots, from somewhere, if that can help".

She makes a horrible face.

"I imagine, your mind is wondering, about something else, I'm not aware of", he says sadly.

She sighs miserably.

"What good things, will come out of this",..." Never seen good time, since the day I came here".

Both walk up hill, in silence, till they reach, Sami's office. Sami's really trapped by his own perceptions of definitely relating in love with Saba.

Sami, searches inside a big box, to find her a new boot. Looks at her in a smiling face. "I need your shoe wear size, but no other preference of color, since all are black", he says.

"That's fine! It's not a gift either"...." No preference". She responds. He hands her one, without giving her any remark. Saba, tries to take out her old boots.

"I hope it fits me" she says, holding besides her the new boots. She wears the new boot and smiles at his face. "It fits me, exact size".

In a half-joking manner he says, "Is there anything that distracted you other than the boot? She gets curious about his question. "Whatever!"..." What do you mean?"

Not intending to express himself about the love he has to her, he says, "Might be you're not aware of it"...." I mean, if I'm not repeating myself". She remains clueless, of what he's saying.

Mulls his question over and over. Again glances at her face, with a wide smile. "Let's keep our connections"...." Naturally, I'm within the process of loving you, if ever it works.

Saba, stares down at her new boots and throws out the old one, to a hole on the ground, the trash place.

Two weeks later.

Anna and Asli are at Anna's home. For Anna, it's all a surprise, to meet her again.

"It's good to see you, safe and alive", Asli says, remembering the awful days of war. Anna, pauses for seconds.

"There I was thinking all about you",... "oh, this cursed war", Anna voices.

"Don't even mention it, it has already stolen our youth life, Asli says.

"I know, It's a depressing stuff".

Anna, slides the envelope towards her, rushing to read it. Asli, looks at her sideways. In front of her, she opens Saba's letter, reading it silently. In the middle, she reads the name of Sami. Before, she finishes reading, the name Sami, rings like a puzzle to solve. Stares at Asli, for seconds.

"By the way, I was to ask about your son, Sami", Anna asks. "Where is he?" She asks.

"The same place, where Saba is now", responds. "You mean at Sawa training camp? She asks. "Correct", she says.

"When did he leave for Sawa? Again she asks, the paranoia rising in her eyes.

"I guess six months ago, Asli responds, trying to figure out, the details of her questionings.

"What exactly do you know about your son Sami?" "I guess he's a trainer, she answers.

Anna, in her mind connects the dots, "Sami the trainer...her daughter Saba, in Sawa's training camp! "It's good news both of our children", are together, in the same unit, she says, raising from her seat.

"This's another good news, if it materializes, according to our wishes, though I don't know the detail of it.

Caffe.

An Old Italian man, his name Giuseppe, in his early seventy, is together, with his old friend Gianni, sitting in small cafe, in Asmara the capital city. Both are chatting in Italian language, about their old experience of war in Africa.

"Asmara Asmarina la piu bella di tutti", (Asmara Asmarina, the beauty of all), exclaims, sipping his hot, "caffe-late", (coffee with milk). Gianni, stirring his black coffee, "Devo dire, che Asmara e solo per gli Asmarini, punto", (I have to say, that Asmara is for the Asmarini, period), not exaggerating on his part.

Giuseppe, pauses for seconds, again taking a sip after a sip. Looks at him, reading on his face, "E un guaio non adattare a questa meravilliosa cultura" (it's pity, not to adopt, to this marvelou culture) he says, opening a pack of cigarette. The eagerness they have, to know about old colonial time.

"Desidero, che invece di colonizare il loro terreno, colonizare il cuore del popolo", (I wish we colonized the heart of the people, rather than their land). Waiting for further explanation. " Ti senti colpevole?" (Do you feel guilty?). Asserts his opinion. " Certo!" (Of course I do!)

Sawa training camp.

Sami six feet tall, with a well-built athletic body and his Afro-style hair, comes out from his little tent, with his pistol at his right belt. He whistles three times, as all 12 military trainee, rush to the place. All sit under a big tree. Lowers his hat down, looking right and left. Grins.

In a loud voice, he shouts. "Welcome! Eritrea forward!" All respond.

"Victory to the masses!"

He starts to call, each by their proper name. As he reads Saba's name he stops for seconds, his whole body and mind admiring the beauty of Saba. Again gives them the initial military instruction.

"From today on, it is mandatory",... "to call you by your nick name only" he says.... "So choose any nickname you have".

All one by one report their nicknames.

When he reaches Saba's turn, abruptly stops, immersed in excitement, seen her beauty.

"What's your nickname, the beauty of her mother?" He asks, his eyes fixed, still on her eyes.

"Guess what!" I don't have any nick name, she says leaning forward. Saba finally, meets his look, mildly smiling. Sami, sees the deep worry in her.

"If you don't have it!"... "How about if I give it to you?" He asks. Though not liking, of any new nickname, to be given by anyone, she says, "feel free!"... "I am under your order!" she responds, trying to hide her feeling, with a trembling smile.

Sami, stares at her, moving his eyes left and right. "If you give me the green light",... "I'm ready to give you one", he says, glancing at her. Saba nods. Takes a deep breath.

"Which one!" she asks.

Sami, not smiling, he suggests, "SAWA!"... "Just to rhyme with your name, Saba".

"I like it!"... "But do I deserve to be called by that name?"

The next day.

When it is dark, Sami invites Saba, to his office. Both sit on an old chair, facing face to face. He looks up at her, kind of smiling, "Oh, you are here on time" he says, in his mind thinking, about the previously discussed, the discipline issue.

"An order is an order!"... "Just tell me, what'll my damage to discipline be!" She says, sitting up straighter.

"I hope you bare with it!" He says, looking at her and trying to laugh.

"I'm tired",... "I better just leave you, for now", she sighs.

Sami, looks at her for a long moment, "Okay don't get upset",..."Here's the deal" he says, exchanging a long look in between. "Ten push-ups",..." Ten sit-ups" and "One mile jogging".

"I can handle it", she responds, breathing lightly.

Both walk outside, side by side to a River bank. After they reach, a green grass with flower bed, Sami, invites her to sit on the grass. Cutting a bunch of flowers and putting it on one side.

"How, if I propose you, another kind of discipline?" He smiles. Her mouth is slide open, searching her head, thinking what kind of proposal might be.

She sighs, "tell me what your proposal is?" I wish I know what you're thinking about, she adds. They look at each other. Rubs, the back of his neck and says, "I mean, just substituting, the discipline of war, to the discipline of love", he says, arranging the flowers.

She bites her lips. "I'm kind confused".... "Be clear, of what do you mean, my dear trainer".

In a whisper tone, he says, "I mean, I am in love with you!"... "As I am training you, how to win a war, on your part, you have to train me, how to love".

Takes a deep breath, looking at him sternly.

"War and love don't go together!"... "But let me follow you!... "I'm kind anxious to see the deal!

Stares at her, with a serious face. "Here is the deal!"... "Ten kisses",..."ten hugs", one mile walk with me.

Taken back to a deep thought, laughs weakly.

"Then what? She says, tracking the ending, before she's to agree with his deal. Hurries back into his own conclusions. "You will end up, to be my lover and wife!" he says. Tracks back about all his moves.

"How about my military discipline?" She asks.

"You will be forgiven, for the exchange of love", he responds.

The next night.

When it is dark, Sami invites Saba, to his office. Both sit, on an old chair, facing face to face. He starts to talk, about the previously discussed, the discipline issue. "Oh!

You are hear on time!", he says, looking at her kindly. "An order is an order!" Just tell me, what will my damage to discipline be! "I hope you bare with it!" looking gravely into her eyes. "I will try!", she says, wrinkling her nose. "Okay" he says, just turning to her, spilling it all out. "10 push-ups, 10 sit-ups, two miles of jogging, one climbing the hill and going down. "I can handle it!" she says, needing no time to think.

Both walk outside, step, side by side. After they reach a green grass with flower bed, Sami, invites her to sit on the grass. He cuts a bunch of flowers, putting it on one side.

"How, if I propose you, another kind of discipline? He says, stretching his hand, with a bunch of flowers. Pauses for seconds.

She smiles, waiting for his say, how it concludes.

"Just, substituting the discipline of war, to the discipline of love", he says, his eyes shut, feeling her watching him. "I am kind confused", she responds, concentrated solely, on his views. "Be clear, of what do you mean, my dear trainer", she adds, feeling a bit nervous.

"I mean, I am in love with you!"... "As I am training you, how to win a war,"... "on your part, you have to train me, how to love". Takes a deep breath, looking at her, in a stern look.

"War and love don't go together!"... "But let me follow you! I am kind anxious to see what the deal is!" she says giving him an empty look.

Stares at her, with a serious face. "Here's the deal!" Leans back to her ear.

"Just move on", Saba says, glancing back at him.

Sami looks her straight in the eye. "Ten kisses, ten hugs, one mile walk with me and-,

Interrupts him, taken back to a deep thought. "And then what?", she says.

"Let me track the ending, before I offer my deal". Hurries back into his own conclusions.

"You will end up, to be my lover and wife!"

Tracks back about all his moves. "How about my military discipline?" She asks, trying not to resist, his pleas and offer. You will be forgiven, for the exchange of love! He says, ending the conversation.

Two days later.

Saba, is washing her cloths, at a river bank, Sami sneaks from behind. He stretches both of his hands, he covers eyes.

"Guess who's behind you?" Sami asks, waiting for her guess, impatiently.

Saba, tries to struggle, to uncover her eyes, from his hands, pleading Sami.

"UN familiar voice! Please uncover my eyes", she says seriously.

Still covering her eyes, hiding his breath, in a whisper, he says, "I will let you if you only guess it".

Holding his both hand with her hand, tries to free her eyes. "No more for a second guess! Reveal yourself".

He uncovers her eyes. Hands extended.

"It is me, Sami, your trainer", he says, grabbing her arms and looking her in the eyes.

Sami, sits beside her, on a rock at the river bank. Faces towards her, smiling. He chuckles.

"Yes your trainer!"

Saba smiles and slides her hand down sis arm.

"There you're!"...."How I may help you my dear trainer?"

He smiles. "Help me to be your lover!" he says, lowering his voice.

"Your lover! Your lover! I am kind lost!"

"Let my issue stay for later!" Sami says, pounding his way out.

Sami, the next day of the training day, he wakes up early in the morning, with Saba being in his mind. Though he has no idea, on how to win her, as his lover, to allow a woman, in his life, to be his wife, that day he kept wondering in his mind. As he whistles three times, all the trainee, rush towards the field, except, Saba being late 10 minutes.

Sami, as he sees Saba, running towards the field, in his mind thinking, on how to discipline her and at the same time, not to lose the future, of being her lover, not to embarrass her he smiles halfway.

Gives her a long stare, looking at her undone hair. Chuckles. "I see your hair is not done".

Feeling unexpectedly shy, glances at him side way. "Nods".

With a firm statement, knowing, the issues of female involvement, in the military service, not very accommodating, chuckles, "No hair braiders at our camp".

Saba, grins, "I know! It is not the right place". "Well, all's true". Instantly, Saba engages her mind, to

recall her mother's experience, during the armed resistance. Though one third of the Freedom fighters, all were females, they were not in the position of being in the leadership.

"Well, for too long, the revolution choked, the females right, to be in the leadership", she says, her eyes getting wide. Sami, stares at her. She keeps talking. "You know, the What? How? And the why? Of it.

"I know", he says, holding up his hand over his head crossed. "I've thought about this",... "I know it's not ideal, not to consider females involvement", he adds.

All trainees are playing soccer, not minding about Sami and Saba who're sitting alone, not far from the field. A kicked ball lands, near them. One of the trainees, rushes to recover the ball. Moves to pick it up, looking at both sideways. "The new beginnings", he says, in a low voice dribbling, the ball in his hand. Saba shakes her head, while Sami gazes at him curiously. He leaves them running to the field.

Sami shrugs, making sure to avoid the trainees comment. Saba, shot him a curious look.

"I've enough of these gossips" she says, shaking her head left and right.

"Gossips don't change life either" he responds back.

"For me it's hard enough".... "Do you know, what's going to do with my life? She voices, gazing at his face.

He reflects for seconds, thinking about how every single responsibility, is going to be on his shoulder.

"Well, for now let's focus, on things we control, rather with peoples gossips" he points out.

She looks at him. "You don't have to tell me, about that?" She says, getting serious.

He shrugs, trying to look less worried. "It's going to be okay", he says keeping his voice low and convincing.

Sami whistles two times, as the trainees stop playing, all running towards their tents. Sami orders all to stay in their respective places.

Sami invites Saba to go with him to his office. Saba follows him, stepping slowly. Her mind still hanging up, to all love affairs, he's projecting, she sits across him. He's, more interested, in the beauty of Saba, to make his wish feasible. Instead of, directly asking her, approaches her mind, in a tricky way. Blinks his eyes.

"Are you avoiding..."

"Avoiding what?" she interrupts him. "My hanging out with you?" he sighs.

"I'm trying to avoid it".... "That's not my style"....

"Especially with the way you're acting, I don't feel good."

"Maybe you're right" he says, feeling the feeling of not to lose the future.

She gets silent for a moment, thinking, she can't find a way through it. He watches at her face from across, shrugging his shoulder like a trainer.

"I don't have much energy, trying to avoid it", she says, touching her Afro hair.

"If I were you I wouldn't act like that", he says.

Saba takes a longer look on his face, gazing at his face. "Eventually, I've to tell you something", she says. He looks at her kindly. "It's tough for me, to continue with this love affairs of your agenda" she says.

"I know" he replies, trying to step out. He steps back and gasps. "You know, to be engaged in love, Sawa's not the right place", she says, trying to look down on him.

He "Nods".

"This's my life, a military life", she adds.

"No need of any explanation" he says, turning around and eyeing her cautiously.

Military graduation day.

All through the training time, keep busy with their academic classes and the military training, side by side, till the round is to end. A week before they are to be discharged from the camp, most of the trainees got chance, to meet their peers and class-mates. And then the day of the graduation comes. Some of them are so excited...nervous....upset or happy. On the eve of the graduation day, a mile away, from training camp, a shootout, between the Rashaida and the Sawa patrol unit, is heard.

Sami's unit are all together entertaining their last night of training. Suddenly, Sami orders, all his unit, to be ready.

All hold their guns on their shoulders, taking their positions. Sami, watches the surrounding, with his binocular, on his eyes, in a relaxed mood. The gun battle it lasted only several minutes.

"Be calm! The situation is in our hand", Sami voices in louder tone. A Trainee One, not convinced of the situation, "What do you mean?", he asks.

Sami clears his throat, again staring at all, calmly, "Everything is under control", he repeats.

A Trainee Two, his eyes fixed to Sami, "What really happened?" he asks.

"'Two of the evil Rashaida are apprehended."

"Damn Rashaida!" Saba shouts. "By the way who are they?" she adds. Sami, gasps, never having anything nice to say about them. "Are they Eritreans?" She inquires. Sami, gives her a satisfying look. He nods.

"They're Arab looking Eritreans", Sami responds.

She raises her arms above her head. "So why do they commit all atrocities to their own compatriots?" Saba asks.

"I listen you!"..."All things ain't right with them politically."

"I'm feeling hate, with these Rashaidas", she voices in a loud tone. Both exchange some horrible awkward moment, not saying anything for long seconds.

Plan of an escape.

Sami and Saba are discharged from the military. A frightening thought, comes into her mind. Immersed in a deep thought, thinking about her childhood friend Yoni, who died when she was six years old. Talks to herself loudly, thinking about his smile, laughter and Angelic look.

"Yoni! Yoni! At least you are rejoicing",... "up in heaven", and "it's good for you". That's why our fathers say, "The world's is Nine, never completes Ten.

Sami is sitting on a chair next to Saba, just entertaining himself reading the news-paper. At that moment, while reading, on the column, of the military section, suddenly, interrupts reading, throwing the newspaper besides him.

"Ah, what kind of life it's". He says talking to himself, in a low voice.

He's kind bothered when he reads, about the military recall, the regime has announced.

Not knowing, of what's going on, in her mind, suddenly, Sami intervenes gently. "Hey darling!"... "What's going on with you? He says, getting quite for seconds. "By the way who's this Yoni, you're much preoccupied, about?" He adds.

Saba steps over to him, where he is sitting, looking at him, until her eyes get misted with tears. "Is nothing Honey"....

"He's my childhood boyfriend, who died of meningitis" she responds, not holding it secret, much longer.

Sami, glances at her, with a smile, in Saba's tear-filled eyes. "Okay, let's never have, any secrets between us"....

"All right darling?"

Prearranged Marriage.

Saba, falls into a deep sleep. Her breath dies and her mind, dreaming, concentrates on the love life, she passed with Sami, at Sawa training camp.

Anna, steps towards her, as she hears a loud scream. She stands besides her bed, pressing her hand against her chest. Her heart is still pounding.

Few minutes later she moves to the dining room, just to hear a light knock at the door. Immediately she steps towards the door, trying to open it, not knowing whose behind the door. Three male Elders, from the neighborhood, standing still, they wait for her offer, to let them in. She looks around, just to check, if no one is behind them. Once, she made sure of the surrounding, invites them to get in. All step in greeting her, sitting around the dining room table.

"You seem very uncomfortable", says, one of the Elders, who's sitting in the middle, smiling lightly.

"Good reading",... "I was just scared of the regime's secret services", she says, turning her face towards them, with a smile.

"I feel you, this time, everyone, is under the fear, of the security secret services", he responds, looking at her eyes.

"What brings you here?" She asks, blinking her eyes, for seconds.

All, get silent, facing each other. Suddenly, one of the Elders, raises up, to give her a feed back, the reason, of their visit.

In a low tone, "If you have time, we're here for an important reason", he says, looking straight at her eyes. She remains silent, not saying anything.

"We just came for one reason", he says. "For what reason?" She asks.

The hard talk, to make it easy, "we're here, simply to make a cultural request", he says, not delving into the issue.

Lingers in her mind, thinking of what the cultural request, might be.

"If you're willing, or thinking, your daughter to get married",... "we're ready",... "for an arranged marriage".

The house gets real quiet, for seconds. She approaches him, with cleaning question.

"My daughter to marry with whom? She asks, politely, looking down to the floor.

One of the Elders, the father of a diaspora guy, raises from his seat and tries to engage, politely. He says, "if all gets right",... "it's my son who will be marrying your daughter".

Her mind, suddenly gets irritated, thinking about Saba, who's already, engaged in love, with Sami.

Gets into argument, like annoyed, by this secret, of prearranged marriage. Makes a quick glance at them, looking with uncomfortable look.

Sighs, "I disagree, with all your secretive deals", she says. As our fathers say, "Is better the devil I know, than the Angel I don't know" she adds, sticking to her views. "Personally, I hate the prearranged marriage".... "Your good thought, might only become a novel".... "Accept the challenges, of the new generation",... "rather than acting, by the holy culture you grew up", she voices, like preaching them.

All the Elders, leave the house, silently, stepping out, not talking to each other. A while after, One of the Elders, re- reads the brief experience of the dialogue.

"The Freedom fighter, they do straight talk, they don't care, who's who", he says, feeling uneasy.

The other Elder, responds, "It's not our creation, but we were following our culture".

The Diaspora's guy father, says, "all blessings, shower from up-down",... "well, though we didn't succeed, her view should be respected".

Honeymoon.

Sami and Saba, plan to go for their honeymoon, being in a hotel room, earlier on the day. Dahlak islands, is their first choice. Early in the morning, Saba, gets up from her bed, to make ready, all their needs. She's busy walking back and forth. Suddenly, she opens the window curtain up to the ceiling. From far, she sees, a little motor boat, running slowly towards the Hotel embankment. Sami is still sleeping.

"Honey! Honey get up please",... "the owner of the boat, is down loading People", she says, standing besides the bed.

Sami struggles to open his eyes, rubbing his face with his hands, yawns. Wakes up and runs to the bathroom, just to wash his face, not taking any shower. In rush not to miss the boat, both walk down the stairs, each carrying the back bag.

The boat's on a stop position, but still the motor running. The boat Man, viewing the riders, offers to each a smile, greeting all, by saying welcome. He starts the motor. Grins. "Ready Guys"?

The boat starts to move, first in slow motion, then speeding. Saba is enjoying the environment, as Sami is half asleep, gasping and yawning, leaning on the shoulder of Saba. "Don't you see, how gorgeous, the landscape of the Island, is? She says, keeping her eye on the water. Sami, yawns, deeply thinking about his dream, the night before their departure.

"I'm stolen by my inside, no more to admire the nature", he says, rubbing his face with his hands.

Saba sighs, "I guess, you had a bad night?" She says.

He "nods", looking at her side way. Turns her head, towards his front, looking face to face.

Sigh, "I can read it on your face". Reviewing, in his mind, the bad images, of his dream.

"Yes, I had a bad dream".

Saba, pretends, to examine, the label of his preoccupations. "What did you dream about?" She asks.

Puts his arm around her. "I saw, an image of a boat sinking and people drowning".

Asli's home.

Asli, on her own, is sitting on chair, being out on the compound, enjoying, the early summer whether, before the rain season is to come about. Sami shows up, walking inside, stepping towards her. She silently approaches him. In her mid-age sorrow and unhappiness radiating on her face, as she sees her son, she greets him, wiping her face with a white cloth. Being aware of the social and political transitions, happening inside the country, she doubts about all her sacrifices, she paid.

"Is this, the freedom, that our children expected", she murmurs, as it turns to be slavery.

Putting the white cloth, back into her pocket, she glances at him. "It's hard when things end like this",... "when no one is responsible, for all the desertions, to unknown land", she says, talking to herself.

Sami as he observes, his Mom, is soaked in affliction and desolation, just talking to herself, stands before her.

"I've nothing left here, except you Mommy", he voices, trying to console her.

"I see all your reasons",... "fleeing the country",..."my mind don't accept",..."just to leave us in a shadow, she says. "By the way how are your plans running? She asks.

With his emaciated face smiling weakly, responds, "fine",... "just beating the last stroke of the drum". Again fixing her eyes towards her son. "Did you foresee the advantage and disadvantage of your decisions?"

"Definitely, I know it is going to cost me". Caresses his face, near his ear in a whisper. "Did you share your plan with Saba?"

"Not yet",... "I still made it secret to her".... "I'm still investigating her position'.

"Do it diligently",... "since she is a female, she could easily be hurt".

"I'll do my best to convince her".... "I hope it works for me, Mom".

You better, coordinate it well". "It'll only work, if you can show her, another paradise better than your place.

The decision of an escape, on his part, though, there's no hindrance, for Saba, it remains, UN climbable, cliff. One last time, he tries to convince Saba, to accept his plan of an escape, without telling her detail of it.

That day, both meet at a small coffee shop, in down town. Before to enter, his main issue, of a plan of an escape, distracts her mind, with another one.

"How did you find our honeymoon?" He asks.

"It was wholesome, I can't, actually reconsider, another one, she responds, excitedly. Goes back, to the main issue. Trying to put her in his power, he grins, "If you don't mind, I want to tell you, something".

Saba, holds her ear, close to his mouth. "What's it? She asks.

"This time", you're immigrating, with me, he says fixedly looking at her eyes. Shakes her head, as though she has not understood, his position. "Whatever that may be, I am kind worried".

"Worried about what?" "About my Mom, she responds.

"Same I'm too worried about my Mom, he says.

"But, you know my Mom is disabled, she only count on me, she sighs.

"By the way, where to escape, Darling?" She asks. "Where our feet leads us", he responds.

"How did you find our honeymoon?" He asks.

"It was wholesome".... "I can't, actually reconsider, another one", she responds, excitedly.

Goes back, to the main issue. Trying to put her in his power, he grins. "If you don't mind, I want to tell you, something". Lifts her head up, holding her ear, close to his mouth. "What's it?" She asks. "This time",... "you're immigrating, with me"", he says fixedly looking at her eyes.

Shakes her head, as though she has not understood, his position. "Whatever that may be, I am kind worried".

"Worried about what?"

About my Mom, she responds. "Same I'm too worried about my Mom", he says.

"But, you know my Mom is disabled",... "she only count on me", she sighs. "By the way, where to escape, Darling?" She asks.

"Where our feet leads us, he responds".

The smuggler.

The awaited date, of a plan of an escape is nearing. That day Sami, spent his time, at a famous Tea shop in Downtown, trying not to think of his awful military experience at Sawa camp. He's just, waiting, meet the camel man, Mr. Ali, to arrange a deal of an escape to Sudan. He decides not to loiter outside, sitting on his own, at the corner. He feels, okay, with the deal he made with Saba, earlier.

Mr. Ali, is rushing, walking towards the Tea-shop, being late at the scheduled time.

"Sorry for being late" he says, sitting at a chair, facing across Sami.

"I expected it, you're going to be late", Sami responds, in teasing tone, chuckling. Sami, orders another round of tea.

"So you really decided to desert the country?", Mr. Ali asks. "Actually yes" he responds, closing his eyes.

"It's unbearable, even to think to live her", he adds.

"I know what you mean and I know how it feels", he says, nodding vigorously.

"If you don't mind, let's go straight to the deal", Sami voices.

He has only to think about it for seconds. "It's camels ride", all the way breathing the fresh air", he chuckles.

"I know that".

"You have only to bring, a rain protection stuff, with raw and dried bread".

"I know what you're asking in dollars, but what'll be in local currency?"

"One thousand five hundred for one". "I hope you don't say to anyone".

"Secrecy is my profession, don't worry about that"....

"that's how I run my business".... "If I do it then I will inflict the danger to myself".... "I keep my word".

An hour later, Sami's riding his bicycle, back towards home. On his way, in the middle his bicycle breaks. He goes down. "It sounds my bike is broken" he says. Struggles to put the chain back to its place. "I hope everything goes well"....

"It looks like a bad luck". Again he rides his bike. Suddenly, as he sees sideways, he sees a military guy, with his uniform.

Briefly, exchanges an easy look with the military guy. "I don't want, to get caught, by the regimes soldiers, to be in jail for indefinite time of my life", he says, looking up the sky, through the haze.

Saba is sitting outside the door stairs, giving her back to the evening sun's rays. Sami, locking his bicycle around a tree trunk, he greets her.

"Everything is ok with you Saba?"

Her face turning to red, tears running down her face, in a low voice she also greets him.

"I'm fine".

Lifts her up, like a baby on his/her mothers chest smiling on her face. She mumbles.

"Honey, what is going with you?"

Picks up the notice letter, from her pocket and shows it to him.

Sighs. "As we struggle to live",... "there comes the trouble, that drives away our blessings" and happiness", she says.

He lays her down on the ground. He only has to think about it, for a minute, then starts to read the letter, making a horrible face.

"This time I'm one step ahead of the ruling party (PFDJ). Figuring out, what the solution might be, he Gasps.

Both step inside the house. He sighs. "An endless war"! Another sigh. "No one took it seriously, making our life hard to live".

"What's the solution Honey?" She smiles. He sighs.

"The solution is one",... "though I don't know the ending, nor the beginning".

She raises her eyebrows significantly towards him. "Honey" she whispers,... "I know that it feels sad", she says.

"No other choice, besides fleeing the country, he says, morosely. She starts to cry quietly.

"I don't want to leave you alone", he says, looking puzzled.

Blinks her eyes with her innocent face. "I understand of what we are going through, if you can't fight better to flight.

"I'm looking for a place, where to be safe".... As our fathers say, "Either do what they tell you, or leave the country for them", she sighs, gazing at herself.

The night before their escape, Sami and Saba are together in the house. Saba, is braiding her hair, doing it herself.

Sami, sees her half-way braided.

"Wow, now you look very original."

Saba smiles. "What'll, the next appreciation be, after I complete my hair braiding?"

"Nothing new, but repeating myself!"

Sami sits on a chair, gazing at her and contemplating Saba's beauty. After a couple of minutes, completes her braiding.

"I hope you like my braiding?"....

"The bread that will satisfy me, I know it, while it is on the oven", as our fathers say...." So definitely yes". He responds.

"What to mean?" Saba asks.

He smiles, trying to explain his say. "You are naturally beautiful!"... "Without adding the other stuff",... "I mean- the women's beauty spices".

She twists round, just to show her dress. "I really love you Sami! Born only to praise!"

She goes back to her packing. Sami goes to his bedroom. Lies on his bed, not really attempting to sleep. His eyes widely open, enters into a deep thought.

"How it would feel, if ever we're caught on our way? He struggles, tossing and turning on his bed, trying to find comfort.

Farewell.

Saba organizes, a farewell party, at her house, inviting her family members, and some other friends, without openly revealing, the issue of their plan. All, are having a good time, as they're enjoying, the traditional coffee celebration. Anna, is brewing coffee, sitting on a stool, and Zaid, Saba's aunt, is making ready, all the coffee utensils. The kids are playing, local games out door.

Six years old Bettin, being in front of all, he tries to dance, with the beat of drum, emitted from the tape-recorder.

"Wow", says Anna, as he's twirling and shaking his neck, left and right. All clap at him.

Zaid, sighs. "For all our children, I doubt that all our laugh, is like a cry to them".

"Further explanation!"... "My dear, for the one you throw, on the floor", Anna asks.

"I mean we can't communicate, with them easily", Zaid responds.

"Totally I agree with you, Zaid", Asli says.

"Hmm. Don't over complain, I hope our presence, with affection is enough", Anna intervenes.

Bettin, again, sneaking through the door, steps towards Anna, who still, is busy brewing the first round, of "Bereka". He twist all his body, acting like Hip-hop dance, finally to kick the coffee pot, "Jebena" to the ground.

All get surprised by his action. Anna, tries to calm Bettin and cool down the situation.

"Come here!" Bettin, the king of the Jebena".

Zaid, Looks at her son, seriously with a stern face.

"Your son, has to go to Sawa", Asli says jokingly.

Zaid, frowns. "May your mouth be filled, with dogs shit", replies seriously.

Asli, grins. Laughingly, leans towards her and says, "Just to change his behavior".

Zaid, feeling bad, she replies. "Instead, of wishing him the holy places!" To Sawa!

Saba and Sami move out, stepping towards the main compound gate.

"Did you enjoy the party?" he says grinning at her face.

"Somewhat!" responds, thinking, about the worst part of their plan to escape. He doesn't feel at ease at her response. He sighs. "That didn't sound good", he says, looking concerned.

"You see",... "I'm about to lose my Mom", she says, never to be able to smile again.

Leaning towards her ear he smiles. In a whisper tone, "I hope you're ready, for the journey?"

Looks at him with her mouth wide open. "In my mind, not really!"... "You don't bless the king, just wishing the opposite",... "I mean not to immigrate".

"What do you mean?" he asks, fearing she might not accept the plan.

"Though I will join your plan unwillingly",... "I can't do the opposite, otherwise".

He gasps. "War and Love don't go together, as sorrow and happiness, and we are not Angels".

The night of an escape.

It's half an hour to mid night. Sami and Saba get ready, waiting for Mr. Ali the camel man to show up, in minutes. Looks at her, reading her mind, not saying anything.

"How're we going, to cover the journey, to the border?" She asks. He stops still, for seconds, before to give her an answer. Glance back at her, following the shock on her face. "Our journey will be riding a camel" he says, slightly, turning away his face.

"I don't feel comfortable, with camels ride", she says, shaking her head, left and right, feeling miserable.

"I'm sorry", he says, not to let it, turn into an argument. "The only means to do it, it's through the traffickers",... "there's no other way", he says, shutting his eyes.

It's mid-night. Mr. Ali's on time, with two camels, standing outside. He manages, to order the camels, to sit in a sitting position and steps towards the house. Sami, hears the sound of foot-steps, It's Mr. Ali. Right away, he opens the door.

Mr. Ali is standing right in front of the door.

"Welcome", Sami says, in a low voice.

"Are you ready, you guys? Says in a whisper.

Sami steps out, while trying, looking back, to see if Saba's following him. After few minutes, Saba leaves the house, walking in tip-toe.

Stares at Saba.

"Is it your first time to ride a camel?" Mr. Ali asks, putting on, his torch towards the sitting camels.

"My first", she sighs.

"Camels ride, it's not like a car ride", he voices, in a low tone.

She "nods".

He gives them, a brief instruction. On how to ride a camel. "You know, when a camel raises up from a sitting position",... "it makes two moves, one forward and the second back ward",... "so your body has to act, the opposite", he explains. Saba looks at him frowning, for a long moment. "Just follow me" he says, riding on the lead camel. Sami and Saba ride on the second camel, acting the same way, like Mr. Ali.

The journey to the Sudan border, starts right away. Mr. Ali leading them in a total darkness, one more time looks back at them.

"Until we leave the town", no one is allowed to talk", he advises. After half-hour, they disappear from the town.

Eight hours onto their ride, early in the morning, they see from a distant, a colony of monkeys, entertaining near a river Barka. Saba, in fear, without lifting her eyes, from the monkeys, grabs the upper body of Sami.

"Here again" she yells, trembling her body. She keeps squirting, her face with Sami. Sami, gazes at her, smiling mildly. "I see, you're making this up", he says.

"What do you mean? She asks.

"I mean, still you're with your old fears". She looks at him frustrated. "Are you kidding?

"I never certainly, mean to suggest that", he says.

Two days after their departure, crossing mountains and plain lands, they're about to reach their destination. One kilometer remains to reach the border. It's night in complete darkness.

"Done with the camel's ride" Mr. Ali says, leading his camel, to sit on a sitting position. Saba and Sami act the same.

All stay under a big tree. The deal of the transaction is done in dollars.

"Beware of the evil Rashaida", the human traffickers, he pronounce, furrowing his brow.... "After you cross the border",... "you have an hour walk, to reach your destination",... "the refugee camp", he instructs.

Shakes his hands and wishes them a good wish.

Left on our own.

They pass the first checking point, just sneaking, through the barren semi-desert land. After half an hour walk, from distant, they hear a shooting from far, though not aiming at them. Saba, lays down on the sand, covering her head, her body trembling.

"Honey", are they shooting towards us?"

Sami, tries to sit down near her, on the sand and calm her. "Not to us, might be to other unlucky, Eritrean escapee", he respond.

Shrugs his thick shoulders, hiding his internal emotion of been fearful.

"It's better to stay here, for a while", he says   "The

human Animals, the Rashaida, usually they perform their evil act during the day time", he adds, leading her to a bush tree to hide themselves.

It's, five o'clock in the morning, two hours before the sun is to rise up. They're half-way to their destination. Saba gets tired of walking. Enters into a deep thought, turning away her back.

"I hope we reach our destination, without being victims of the Rashaida", she says.

She is very worried, about their safety, from this merciless cruel traffickers, but on the other hand, she felt the security, by being near to Sami. Mixed emotions radiate across her face, battling the battle of two wills, that of following her lover Sami and the advice of her Mom. She tries to review, her love experience, with Sami at camp SAWA military training.

"Honey!"... "You're a wonderful man! "You, too are generous darling!"

A few minutes later, memories of her love affairs, with Sami, runs in her mind, as she stands by his side, watching him smile at her face.

She smiles.

"Do you remember?" "Remember What?"

"I mean the discipline, I still have to face, while we were in Sawa.

Ends her thought quickly.

"You mean the ten push-up and sit-ups?

"Yes honey",... "you know words once said, they matter whether for good or for bad".

"Right time to pay it back!"... "You know the deal already, darling!"

"Yes!"... "Ten kisses and hugs".

Entertain, their hugs and kisses, glaring at each other. Sami, suddenly, feels a feeling of regret and forwards an act of apology, fighting back his tears, beating his chest. "Culpa mea",... "if anything, happens to us, I am responsible".

"If ever we pass this dangerous time, It'll all remain a distant memory",... "now time to sleep".

Saba caressing his hair, returns a smile to Sami. Sami falls asleep. She sits down and watches her surroundings.

Anna's Home.

It's almost six month, since the beheading of thirty six East-African the majority being Eritreans. Anna seated herself, across Grandma and Grandpa, is in a deep thought, thinking about the barbaric act of the ISIS. Grandpa and Grandma, gaze at her without saying anything. Anna, looks down to her feet, lightly scratching her artificial leg. "Unfortunately, we're not lucky, to hear about the good news", as she sees things escalating from worse to worse. "Umm," says Grandma, fumbling for the tiny coffee cup. Again, she says, "Ugh"...a throaty voice emerging through her clenched teeth. "This country,...Grandpa pronounces, recalling the old times, in comparison, to the present time tragedy. Anna, follows them and gazes without lifting her eyes. Grandpa emits a growling sigh. Grandma, grunted.

Grandma lifts the tiny cup, up near to her mouth, not taking a sip, for seconds.

"At the time of the Turks Empire, our fathers, shed the normal tears", he says, his eyes looking to Anna and Grandma. "How about the Italian colonizers? Grandma asks. Again, recalling the atrocities of the Italians,..."The same normal tears", he responds. "How about this time? Asks Anna. He looks very embarrassed and sighs. "Shedding, the tears of blood!" he responds. "I can just imagine, myself giving my life, for that goddamn, revolution", Anna says. Grandma, can hardly look Anna in the face. For a minute the house get silent, all gazing to each other. "We didn't expect, all these things to happen to our children", Grandma voices, sighing. "We see within our eyes, all their revolution promises, as they turn to slavery," Grandpa ventures. The house goes unbearably quiet again. Anna, looks at her Grandma. Grandma's eyebrows go up, her mouth still open, seeming to say something. "I hear all your blames", but..."Unfortunately I'm part of it", she says, showing on her face, the hint of softness beneath her anger.

"Heaven help our grandchildren!" Grandma says, attempting to walk out. Anna, stays seated, while Grandpa follows walking out.

Human traffickers.

The desert dust is hobbling on the air twisting like a snake high on to the sky. The desert strikers, two Rashaida, human traffickers, are on their way, to kidnap humans. To get rest they head towards a dried river bank. Put their tent on the ground, both looking tired lay down, sitting, on a big mat. Rashaida One, rubs his long mustache, with his fingers, moving them like playing a guitar.

"Do you think, Allah will forgive us, for what we are doing?" He asks, weariness flushing over his face. Rashaida Two, answers with a sudden air of complicity.

"I fear we could be punished, for all the killings but-" Rashaida One, throws his head forward.

"But what?"

"Humanly, we are caught, in our own trap, but Allah is forgiving".... "After all, we are not killing animals, but human beings".

Both look at each other. Sighs, "What is done is done! We have to go out-"

"Where to go out?" He asks, squeezing the little plastic bottle, after drinking enough water.

Rashaida Two, chuckles.

"To accomplish the job of kidnapping, of our own brothers".

Few minutes later, both drive their closed pick-up, along the desert. Suddenly, Rashaida One, gets into a thought, while driving a tough drive. He gazes sideway, looking at him on his face. Right away, imagining himself not fearful, delves into a discussion, with him. They're discussing about the dirty business of human trafficking, using human trafficking secret codes.

"Did you catch any birds these days?" Ask the driver. "

I got two female birds, last week", the other guy responds.

"You're lucky! Better female than male!" "Yeah! For females it is easy to catch them". "I hear you! Available for rape too".

Sami and Saba spent half an hour, getting chewed by fear, not to get trapped by the Rashaida, human traffickers.

Suddenly, Saba hears from far, a pick-up truck, coming down the street, nearing towards the bush tree, where they are resting. Shivering all her body, tries to wake up Sami, as he is in deep sleep.

"Sami! Sami!" She shouts. Sami wakes up.

"I see a car coming toward us, we are in trouble, maybe they are, the Ra…shai…da", she says gritting her teeth.

Pulls herself together, as she sees the car stopping. The two Rashaida, coming out, rush towards them, walking with their gun on their shoulder. Saba, shouts and yells.

"Oromay" that is the end.

The two Rashaida, pointing their gun to them, they order them, to lie down, facing their face, to the ground. Sami looking at them in distress, he disobeys. Saba, in a chocking voice, "Please don't disobey, do whatever they say", she pleads.

Both, start to beat and hit him, with a big stick, till he becomes unconscious. They tie his hand from his back and throw him, at the back of the car, while Saba, is tied and sits in front of the driver. After almost 24 hours' drive, crossing all the desert, they reach Sinai.

Colonel's office.

It's been almost a month since their escape from the country. An Eritrean military Colonel, is inside his office, sitting on an old chair. In front of him, old books and scattered papers, are laid in disorderly manner. A young officer, smoking his cigarette, steps towards the office. He hears a knock at his door. Walks in standing still, not saying anything. The Colonel offers him a seat, to sit down. He's just staring at the messy office, looking right and left.

Again he stares so hard at the Colonel face, as he's busy folding and unfolding files.

After few minutes, taken back from all what he's doing, he gazes at the officer, not smiling. In an angry tone, "Get this mission done quickly?" he says.

The officer grins, "What mission?" In an angry tone.

"That of ordering, Sami's parents to pay the sum of 50,000 Nakfa." Repeats.

In a low and calm voice, "How come, the parents be responsible, for their grown up children?" he says, wondering if he ever get his point.

He yells, "It is my order." he responds, flipping a file down.

Sighs, "Are you out of your mind?" How about the rule of Law?

Colonel, chuckles, "Where there's no law, one makes his own law." He chuckles.

"I hear you",... "When thieves steal your house, you join them stealing."

Colonel, giggles, "Exactly! You got it and nothing to worry about it."

Later in the day, two Military Men, wearing as a civilian, knock the door of Asli's house, as she's doing her chores. One of the Military, bangs the door, with his left hand and holding his pistol on his right.

Yelling, "Open the door! Open the door!"

Asli, sits back, surprised by the extent of the bung. Another yelling follows.

Right away, Asli rushes to the door her whole body trembling. In a low voice, "Who're you?" "Who're you?" she voices.

Again she hears, "Open the door!"

After she stays for a minute on hold, unlocks the door. In a chocked voice, "Hello! Come on in."

Military one, turns his face, like a beast, to frighten her. "Where's your son, Sami?" he yells.

"I don't know!" she responds not feeling fearful. In turn she ventures a question to the Military men.

"I don't know his whereabouts, and don't frighten me.

" By the way do you know with whom you're speaking? She asks. "Say it, who you're to be", he says, gazing at her face.

"I'm an X-fighter for the independence" she responds, looking straight at their faces.

Delivers her a slip of paper of a court date. In a frightening voice "You are summoned, to appear, at the military court."

The military goes away, stepping through the door. She closes the open door, settling her body on a chair. She tried to read the letter, in a dim light, her breathing becoming deep.

She decides, right there, to call Anna, using her cellphone. Anna as she hears her phone ring, she slips out of her bed, steping towards her cellphone laid on the table.

Grabs it. "Hello!" She repeats, astounded, by the senseless military presence.

On the other end, "Hello" Anna responds.

After being silent for seconds, "I'm sorry" to tell you about the bad news, she says, sitting back on the chair. "Few minutes ago, two military men showed in my house, just to disturb my day".... "I'm summoned to appear in court, she adds. Anna, tries to console her.

Gasps. "What a dreadful fate!" Laments, being terrified.

Asli sighs. "Very appalling! Indeed".... "How come, we take the responsibility, of our own grownup children?"

"There'll not be any life, as far as the local Mafias, are in control of our land". She says, sensing a little antipathy.

Sami's Interrogation day.

Sami's secluded from the other prisoners, for a reason, not to plot, an organized crime, against the Bedouin. They put him, in a lone cell, inside the compound. Sami physically, with a full-figured body, 6 feet tall, Afro hair and with a strong facial features, he looks like a killer, being the most feared by the Bedouin Guards. The Bedouin boss slams the door, of the prison cell behind him. Without looking right or left, he marches straight towards Sami, who is sitting with a shackle on his hands and feet.

The Guard, "Yells", in a voice, he thought, to make himself bold. Kicks Sami's legs, punching his face.

"You black Habesh", he shouts again, sternly, looking at his face. Suddenly, a battle of looks, follows between them.

"If you want to save yourself and your wife, you better pay a ransom of 40,000 dollars", he yells.

Sami grumbling like a bitten dog, he backs to sit down on the ground.

Six hours later.

When the sun goes down, around 6 o'clock in the evening, the Bedouin boss with another Guard, show up, to all the cells. First, he steps, towards the male prison cell.

Saba and Lula, chat, about the unbearable torture, of the Bedouin, sitting and being shackled.

"I can't resist the torture" Lula voices in a weak voice. "No energy to fight it either", Saba responds.

"These Mafia and killers of the desert, they don't possess any conscience".... "May God damn these demons".

The daily torture, all the escapee face, becomes an unbearable situation. Sami, being inside the secluded cell room, he plans a way of an escape. This's what he considered doing. All three weeks, of his stay, kidnapped, under the Bedouin, he digs a small hall under his bed on the ground, burying a plastic bottle, half full of hot green paper. The Eve before the plan of an escape, he mixes the hot paper, with his urine, again returning it, to the hole he dug.

The affliction and the sorrow while back in Eritrea, is still fresh in his mind. "I can't bear, the torture of the Bedouin".

It's a foggy day, the desert dust, hobbles over the area and the compound. Early in the morning, the Bedouin Guard, steps towards Sami's cell. He hardly, bangs at the door. "Yells", looking through the small hole on the door, to see all his movements.

"Wake up! Wake up!" the Guard cries loudly.

Sami is already awake, to make ready to his move, of a plan of an escape. The Guard, steps in. He tries to sit down, on the ground, bowing down to unshackle Sami's feet. Sami's ready, with his plastic, noiseless bomb. He splashes, the bottle of liquid, onto his face.

The Guard, falls back on his shoulder, shouting loudly. "Help! Help!"

Immediately, Sami picks, his gun, from the ground and starts to beat him to death.

The Guard, pleads, waving his hands, left and right. "Please don't kill me".

Sami shackles, the Guard's feet and hand, with the shackle he was shackled.

"The tree is down by itself", he says to himself, chuckling. "Please don't kill me" he shouts again.

"You illiterate the desert gangs", Sami yells.

He looks at his face, "You deserve death", he says wandering back in his mind, the piety and kindness of his people. The Guards heart, starts to beat too fast.

"I come from a disciplined society".... "I'll not kill you if you comply" Sami says looking at him in a stern look.

The Guard looks to the ground.

"Okay, okay Just don't kill me I'll comply". He shuts his big mouth and "Nods".

Right away, Sami wears all the guards cloths, covering all his body except his eyes. Mounting himself, with the gun and some ammunition, slowly and cautiously, walks towards the female's camera cell, where Saba is. In front of the door, from far he sees, another Guard, with his gun, leaning on the wall and sitting down on a bench, smoking his cigar. Sami, slowly, drew up before the Guard and swiftly jumps onto him, knocking him down. The Guard falls on the ground. Sami, repeatedly punches his head and stomach. The Guard, instantly faints down, speechless, blood coming out of his mouth, groaning like a dying goat.

With a knife he opens the door. He steps, with a gun in his hand still covered all his body. Saba, tries to retreat back, her hands shackled. Again she looks at him, without saying anything.

Cries in a low voice.

"Who are you? Who are you?" she says, astounded by the situation. Sami steps further, nearing towards her. Unveils his face, standing in front of her, looking at her intently. She feels a sudden shock, as she bites her lips, her mind shifting in between life and death. Sami leans towards her.

"The Bedouin dance is finished", he says, softly. She steps backward.

"It's me" Darlin, he repeats. Looks at him all over.

"Oh my God! Unbelievable", she says.

Sami unshackles Saba and steps towards Lula. Lula, with a suspected eyes looks at him. She knows Sami by his name only. She learned it from Saba, that he's her husband. Sami unshackles Lula's hands, smiling at her.

"God creates a cliff and at the same time, provides a ladder", she says, contemplating, his bravery and fearlessness.

Sami, hugs, kisses, embracing Saba. Again she touches his upper body.

"Are you really Sami" she asks. "Yes Darling! It is me".

Sami, does the same thing, to save the other male prisoners, who're on the other cameras.

All the detainees, filled with joy and happiness, follow Sami walking behind him. Sami with two guns on his shoulder, moves fast towards the prison compound. There's a parked pick-up, on the compound and the Driver is busy, with unloading foods and grocery for the prisoners.

Sami, approaches behind him, at gun point. He asks the car's key.

"Give me the car's key, or I will blow your head". The Bedouin driver, trembles, in a weak voice.

"Okay, Okay, just don't kill me".

Sami, snatches the key and throws it to Saba. "Quick! Be on a driver wheel", he orders.

Sami and another male, sit at the back, with their guns loaded. Saba, slides on a wheel, as Lula sits beside her, on the passenger side. Saba, starts the Engine, driving on the desert road.

The Bedouin boss, gets aware, of the situation of an escape. He rushes, with his three other Guards, following them. Runs towards his Land-rover in a hurry.

"Stop them! Stop them!" he yells.

"Now they have guns, and the chase will not be easy", he responds, his mind churning with fear.

Bedouin Boss, gets angry. "Do what I tell you, dumb ass".

In the middle, they exchange gun shots. They come near to each other. The driver of the Bedouin boss, is hit on the front head and stops driving. The boss Bedouin takes charge, himself driving very fast, to reach the escapee. Again another bullet strikes the Bedouin boss after which the car stops. Sami, returns walking to the Bedouin truck and he confiscates all their possession's and guns.

Bedouin body.

The Bedouin Boss's dead body before it's to rest, in the middle, his wife, steps towards the cadaver. She pauses, silent not saying anything, for seconds. Remembering the conversation, she had earlier, with her husband, sorrow start to flash in her mind.

She leaves the tent, stepping out with her two kids. Before she starts, talking, to her children, her Daughter initiates the conversation. Crying.

"What happened to our father?" she asks.

"He died of his evil actions, he got his hand", she says, reflecting in her mind, about the devotion she's to give to her kids.

"Why Mom?" asks her son.

"I advised him not to do evil act, but-".

His face looking sad, interrupts her with question. "But what mom?".

Takes a quick intake of breath. "The consequence of being evil, it ends this way".

It didn't help that way, for the Bedouin the desert gangsters, to continue their heinous act of kidnapping innocent people.

Get together.

It's the eve of a cultural and spiritual festivity of "Hoye-Hoye", September 11, (According to Geez right September first). It's the largest annual commemoration, which every Habesha celebrates. It's celebrated under the Patron St. John the Baptist. All twelve months of the year, share equal days of thirty days. To complete the year, the remaining five or six days, are named by "Pagumen", (the last days of the cleansing days). On these days, people go to the river bank, for a bath, (a sign of a spiritual renewal).

There's, the day of celebration. It's a Thanksgiving Day for all Christians, to celebrate, spiritually and culturally.

The sun's going down, behind the mountains. Two hours to go, to start the festivity. When it's completely dark, youths and children, lighting a wooden stick, they marsh along the streets, singing "Hoye-Hoye".

The festivity in its stile, is randomly organized. All neighborhood, of different ages, flock down the street, towards the fire place. One of the Elders, initiates the celebration, by singing a hymn, for forgiveness, from God. A litany of prayers, accompanied by songs follow. Then the Elder, lights the bunch of woods, while all, encircling the fire, on a high flame, dance.

That night Asli's at the place, observing all the cultural and spiritual rituals. She's absorbed and mentally engaged, struggling, between the joy and her life situation, feeling lonely. She stares at herself, reviewing the awful times, during and after the armed struggle.

Eyes exactly, all the rituals, as they were taking place. "Such a pretty culture", she exclaims, silently talking to herself.

When the festivity ended, physically being tired, walks towards her home. Immediately she lies on her bed, not rolling herself to organize it. Six hours later, she wakes up early in the morning, to the sound, of the big Cathedral bells. Her mind starts, to protest and complain, not getting enough sleep. Drinks some water, entering into the very thought, of not being lonely, the day of festivity. Yawns, feeling very tired. Pauses, for a couple of minutes, thinking anything to keep her, the time passing, to fill her day with something. Suddenly, a thought comes to her mind. She plans, to pass it, with her friend Anna.

That very day as her plan, she happens to be with Anna. Asli, getting cautious about Anna's disability, steps to the kitchen, to prepare coffee.

"Any good news about our children? Asks Anna, since she doesn't have any news, about their where about. Asli stares at her.

"If we don't hear the bad news on time, it might be good news", she says.

"I'm thankful, for your surprise visit", Anna says, blinking with tears.

Both exchange an anxious glance.

When the coffee is ready, both sit on the table, to drink their coffee. Unexpectedly, Asli throws an argument, just to distract, Anna's mind, from over worrying. "You know the Habesha coffee is with three F's and three E's". Anna gets confused about her say. Asli, gets a paper and writes, "Cofffeee". Anna gives her a glimpse of smile, getting astounded.

Again, looking around startled, "You're very genuine" Anna says.

The house gets really quiet. Asli, reckons her affliction, reading it from her side. She fixes, the coffee adding milk to it.

Makes first sip, licking her lips, before she's to give to Anna. Anna, feels a little tired, her mind rewinds to the bad memory of the war.

For seconds, she sits there, gripping the tiny cup of coffee, sipping.

"The situation of being separated",... "from our beloved Children, for so long",... "I can't handle it".

"It's strange, even not to hear, about them, all these months" she responds, figuring out, both feeling the same feelings. Asli, believing the cause of their disappointment and pain, being the same.

"I regret for one thing", she says, sucked in deep breath. "For which one? Anna asks.

Takes a deep breath.

"The day, I joined the revolution", she says. "I wish I took the other alternative", she adds. "Which alternative?" Asli asks.

"Engaging my life as a civilian", responds, finding herself lost in regret. Asli, says nothing for a while.

Keeps, trying to sip an empty coffee cup. Looks away, just to stop the negative feeling, she's feeling, in a say.

"A spear thrown and a year gone, never come back again, so don't feel guilty and regretful".

"Thank you for feeling my emotions". "You are welcome".

"Yet, we are not finished".... "We might encounter, other difficulties, on our way".... "Let us face the future and be strong.

PART FOUR.

From Alexandria to Tripoli.

In front of a big Pyramid, in Alexandria, an out door musical show, performed by a single musician is on its way. At the foot of the Pyramid, a man with long hair, with his big hat on the ground, is singing with his guitar, as tourists are giving him some money. It is Sunday late morning, the Mediterranean Sea is quiet and calm, a welcoming sea breath, is refreshing the hot summer day. The street that stretches, before the Pyramid, is full of tourists. One of the tourists, from Virginia state USA, Silvi, is walking on the street, with her small Canon camera on her right, now and then, taking pictures of the environ. As she approaches the Singer, she starts to take some pictures of him. Suddenly, a thief walking behind her, snatches her bag, with all the money and documents.

Looks behind and get confused, yelling, "Thief! Thief!"

The singer, interrupts his singing and steps towards her. "I'm sad and so sorry".... "By the way, did you have money, in your bag?" Gently walks right and left, before where she is standing, after remaining silent, for a couple of minutes.

"Sorry, for being distracted, by my music" he says, seeing the hurt on her eyes. "My music invites, angels from heaven",.... "but believe me, there are always, the evil creatures".

Points out to the Singer eyeballing the area, in distress, in a high voice.

"Hey what should I do now?"

To get her back, to a good mood, bowing down to his hat, picks some coins, on the air. He smiles.

"I share what I have" he says. Delegating, a pleasant look on his face, she smile. "Thank you".... "But I lost all my documents and my ID" she says, still feeling sad about her situation.

"Did you have money in cash?" he says, blowing a frustrated breath.

Checks her pockets, in case she finds some money.

"No, only my credit cards" she responds feeling his generosity, surprised.

"Don't worry!" he says.... "The Island functions, only in cash" he adds. Again, he picks his guitar, backing up towards the stairs.

"Back to my music", he says.

She smiles half a smile, watching the simplicity of the musician, dealing in life with small enough, comparing to the greediness, of her own people.

"Do you have any other job, besides entertaining minds, with your songs?" she asks.

"No", he answers. After seconds of pause, "only part-time". She wonders in silence, not saying anything. Pats her shoulder, briskly.

"I'm alright with the little coins, I get from you, gentle guys".

Silvi, leaves the area, walking down the street, towards the beach. The street's clean. Gets a little bit frustrated, for the fear, not to be again a victim, to anyone. After half an hour walk, there, she steps towards some folks, who're entertaining along the beach. She stops walking, standing still, with fear. After while, proceeds walking, heading towards the group of Sami, who're enjoying the water.

Approaches them from behind, with her Canon photographer, on her shoulder. She decides to join the group, after she looks around, there's no danger. All the group, except Sami, who's still lying on the sand, step towards her, smiling with a happy face. She looks back at them, smiling, as they encircle her standing.

"Who're you? She asks smiling politely.

All, see to each other, staying silent, not to give her an answer. Then Saba looks her in the eye.

"We're refugees from East-Africa", Saba responds, stomping her feet on the sand.

"Where in East-Africa, she asks staring at everybody, in a smile. All get wondering not to mention the name of the country.

"Eritrea" Saba responds.

Keeps quiet for seconds, engaging her mind to figure out, the strange name, she never heard before. "By the way are you Arabs? She asks.

All respond in one voice. "No".

All take pictures with her being in the middle.

Sami is enjoying the scenery of the beach, lying on the sand. Suddenly, in his mind enters into a deep though, making a mental picture of the surroundings and the life under the Bedouin jail.

Saba steps back towards Sami, walking barefoot. Lies beside him. She tries to open her mouth. Sami smiles.

"You miss..." "Miss what?"

"Taking a photo with a stranger white Lady", she responds, looking down to the sand. For a second, he gazes at her, without saying anything.

"Good for you", he says, expecting her to say more of it. She sees, back to his eyes. "I would really appreciate, if you were with us", she says, getting embarrassed.

"Sorry," he mutters to her.... "We're here, not like tourist but refugees," he concludes.

Saba, crosses her arms around his chest, in a loving mood caressing his Afro hair.

"Honey! Honey!"... "May I talk to you… of something very serious?"

Turns his face and glances at her.

"What is going on with you, my sweetheart?" he says, glancing towards the sea waves, running under their feet.

She, enters into a deep thought, that has brought her so much pain and degradation, by the Bedouin boss, as he raped her. She stares towards the water, thinking on how to tell him.

"What a sad life?" breathes out, closing, her eyes and crying like a baby, not knowing where she is.

After a couple of minutes, remembering the awful deeds, of the Bedouin boss, rubs her eyes.

"May I tell you something?" she repeats, her head shaking. He keeps his eyes on her, looking serious.

"Nods."

Her hands and legs trembling. "I was... I was, ra-ra-".

"Say it darling, after all nothing to fear". Tears flowing out on her cheeks.

"I was raped by the Bedouin Boss".

Shakes his head up and down, his eyes turning to red and wide.

"Oh! No!"

The next day.

The next day, they go to a pediatrician doctor, for a possible checkup. The doctor, after he takes blood sample from Sami and Saba, he retreats to his office. Sami sits down on a bench, at the hospital corridor, as Saba sits on his thy, her heart feeling heavy and her mind racing, thinking of the ugly days, under Bedouin Jail.

Most of all, that bothered her is, if the pregnancy is from the Bedouin boss. Bringing back, all her preoccupations, into the present.

Gasps. "If the baby to be born, is not yours,"... "will you still, accept the situation and be my husband".

After, deeply reflecting, on her comment.

"It's bad incident, but I am ready to accept, the reality of it", he responds.

Tears streaming down her face, she hugs and embraces Sami. "It really is a blessing for me, to be your wife".

The Doctor steps out of his office, walking down the corridor, to meet them, as they are waiting, for the result, impatiently, sitting on bench, in the waiting room.

"Congratulation!" the Doctor voice, in a clear and loud tone, looking at Sami in his face. Saba gets over excited, her lips feeling, as though they're forming words. The Doctor, again gazes at Sami, with a smile.

"You are the father of the baby".

Both jump out from where they're sitting, embracing and hugging each other. Sami, takes a good long look, at the Doctor.

He says, "Thank you!" Saba, Kneels down, to the floor, with her hand, stretching high, on the air.

"God be praised!" she shouts.

Journey on the Sahara Desert.

The departure night, from the city of Alexandria, two Libyan human traffickers, drive towards the group, with two big trucks and a pick-up truck. All Sami group are together, waiting out, sitting under an old wooden house. When they arrive, the lead driver honks, several times. All run towards the trucks. The lead Trafficker, standing outside, before the truck, orders all to ride. "Hurry! Hurry!" Make it fast.

Sami, Saba, Jobe and Lula stay together, riding at the back of the open truck. The other remaining, ride on the other trucks. The lead Trafficker, raises his hands up.

"Ready! Let us go!" he says.

Sami's group are chatting and entertaining despite the tough ride. The trucks in full speed, run along the open desert road. Suddenly, a big cloud of dust covers their way.

Lula, touches, the womb of Saba gently, caressing with her fingers.

"Baby boy or girl!" Lula asks, waiting for the echo of her predictions.

"It's a surprise" responds Saba, though she knows, it's a baby boy. "What ever the surprise will be, I hope he/she is born at our dream destination", Asli responds instantly.

Saba sighs. "Let it be, like what your mouth, pronounce!".

Saba, allows herself, another sigh, entering into a deep thought, re-reading in her mind, the day she was born, to be part of this world. Her eyes, get very wide.

"You know I was delivered inside a car" she says. "Ridiculous", she says, her mind resisting, not to accept. Saba continues, "I guess you're surprised".

"Well it's true", she adds.

Lula, surprised, holds up her hands, before she can say, anything else.

"You seem very surprised", Saba says.

"Well, things happen that you don't plan for", expresses Lula, gazing at her smilingly.

On the other corner of the truck, Sami and his childhood schoolmate friend, Jobe, chatting about their past school years.

"Still, the Geography teacher, is in my remembrance",... "especially when he accurately, located countries and places", Jobe says, raising his eyebrow.

"I know it was your favorite subject!" he responds, excitedly. Grins at him. "I hope you practice it now as we escape".

"How?"

"I guess, goggling from your mind, our direction and location!"

Are you kidding? No! I'm serious.

In the middle of the desert, driving in the darkness, all the way, Sami's group stay calm. They only see, the dust hobbling up on the sky. The hot desert breeze, makes all feel bad.

Sami, tries to look around. The truck stops in the middle. All get silent. Suddenly, Sami turns his attention, across the desert, only to see, local people wearing white robs, riding their camels. Jobe, leans over Sami's ear. Sami, stares back at him.

"I hope they're not ISIS", he says, backing up his head from Sami.

Sami looks back at him, raising his head, high above him. "ISIS no more use camels, but big trucks". Gets silent for seconds. "I think they're local people, doing their business", he adds, hoping it's not bad as he thinks.

Six hours later, after a long drive on the desert, all rest under the small bush trees, some lying on the ground and some sitting. The lead Trafficker, steps towards them, to give a further, security directions.

"Well we're not yet at our destination" he voices, in a lower tone.

"All you need's, to be aware and cautious of the surrounding", he adds.

What do you mean by that? Sami asks, feeling all the responsibility, being on his shoulder.

"This place is a dangerous one",..."there're hidden enemies", he says, looking all, turning his neck, three hundred sixty degrees.

Sami shrugs.

"Do you expect to happen something?" he asks. "Maybe, maybe not" responds the Lead Trafficker. He leaves them, walking towards his truck.

Saba not feeling happy, "Who might be the hidden enemy", she asks, sitting near Sami.

"Who ever be" we get to get alert, he responds.

"Okay, so, we're going to alternate, our sleep",... "Half of our group sleep, while the other stay in alert", he voices.

From the opposite direction, the Traffickers, observe, a truck running towards them. "We're in danger!" Says, his binocular fixed on his eyes.

In total darkness, the high beam light of the trucks, is zigzagging, flushing on the white sand. Four, ISIS patrol trucks, moving in line, drive towards them. In a loud voice tone, the Lead Trafficker, directs his Guards, to be alert with their weapons.

"Be ready for the fight! Either we die or they die!" he says, in a loud tone. The Guards move here and there, ready to fight, like taking their positions.

"What is going on?" Sami asks, to one of the Guards. "The ISIS are heading towards us", the Guard responds. "Do you have extra guns and ammunition" Sami asks. "What to do?"

"Whatever! Just to defend our life!" he responds, looking at his face, sternly.

The Guard, looks at him, side way. "Do you know how to operate the gun?"

Of course I know! I was born in war and grew in war!" He responds.

The Guard, leads Sami, towards the Truck. Opens, the back door and hands him one gun with ammunition.

"Here you have!" he say, trembling, trying not to be too scared. Again Sami, stares at him, with a stern face.

"I need ten more guns for my men", Sami voices. "You mean all of you are fighters!" the Guard asks.

Desert Gun battle.

Few minutes later, the ISIS approach near to them. The Traffickers and their guards start shooting aiming at them. The ISIS resisted in the exchange of the gun fire. The shootings get heated and loud.

Lead Trafficker and his Guards, as they see the tense of the battle, they start to retreat, running and leaving Sami, with his men fighting. The battle lasted 30 minutes, Sami's men kill six ISIS, wounding several of them. The remaining ISIS, they start to retreat, driving back their trucks. All Sami's men are safe and no one injured.

Saba and Lula, though not in the fight, for what ever it happens, they are ready, with their guns, being away hundred yards, sitting on hill top. They're just following the on- going battle, following it from a distant.

"The ISIS are retreating", Saba shouts. "I hope our country's Angels are with our men", Lula, responds in a relaxed mood.

"Under our Angels, there is Sami, your brave husband".

The Traffickers and the Guards, come out from their hiding place. Finally, they see the battle is ended. All walk down the hill, in the middle, just to meet, Saba and Lula, who are also going down the hill.

"Really they are very brave men!" says, the Lead Trafficker, glancing at both.

"It's the fruit of their war experience", Saba replies.

They leave, Saba and Lula behind, rushing towards Sami's group.

"I hope, these cowards, they learn a lesson from our men's bravery!" Lula says, feeling a sort of happy.

Sami, is staying, with all his men, near a burning truck of the ISIS. He sits on the sand, crossing his legs with his gun on the ground beside him. The Traffickers and the Guards, walk fast, to reach the group.

Saba and Lula, also reach them, as all are sitting, around the burning truck. Suddenly, they sing, in a high voice, the song of joy, "Elilta" (a sound created between the tongue and the teeth, vibrating). The Guards also carrying water and food, they approach the heroes of the day.

"Honey, I am glad to see you safe and alive!" Saba says, her heart beating fast, focusing, at Sami's prospect, of taking all the risk, to fight the fight.

Sami, inhales deeply. "It's only your mother's prayers and your love that's following me", he says. Saba, surprised by his response, breaths a sigh of relief.

"I'm Proud to be your wife".

Sami, reaching out her hand, kisses her hand. "Honored to be your husband".

The lead Traffickers, steps slowly, towards where Sami is sitting. Impressed, about all their heroism, he approaches Sami, with a big golden medal, ready to award to him.

In a happy face, "I don't have any word to express my joy for your heroism", he expresses.

"Thanks, to the powerful God, who gave us the power", Sami responds. Puts a golden medal on Sami's neck.

"Real heroes from the real land",... "I wish you were my own guards", he voices. Taking advantage of their heroism, "May I hire you and all your brave men?" he adds. "It's a good deal but-"

"But what?"

"We are heading towards the unknown land!"

He sighs. "I wonder how you take, all those risks, to the level of drowning, at the Mediterranean Sea".

"It's not our wish, but forced to flee!"

The Lead trafficker, taking out from his pocket, the exact amount (24,000 dollars), of what they have earlier paid, for their trip fair, hands to Sami.

"Your ride is free" he says, looking down.... "If ever it pays, your heroism, for saving my life" he adds.

"Thank you for your kindness! "It's a great help", Sami repeats.

And then there, all the group, organize UN rehearsed dancing party being under a small tree. Jobe, with his "Krar" (a local guitar), stands, in the middle, playing, as all dance in a circle around him.

Sami, waves his hands, stepping towards the group. With notes of dollars in his hand, approaches them, giving them a big smile.

In a loud voice, "Our ride is free!"... "It's free".

Jobe, interrupts his music. All face towards Sami, as he slowly steps towards them. He leans so close to them.

"On what deal?" Jobe asks.

"On the deal of our heroism", Sami responds. All in one voice.

"Fantastic deal".

Sami and Saba never have chance to exercise their love freely, for a quite some time. When the group leave for a sleep recess, he invites Saba, to step away and entertain with love, being alone from the group, sitting on a big rock. "Darling I missed you for a couple of hours", her arms going about his neck, kissing him.

"Me too!"... "Honey I have to tell you, that I love you so much!"

"I trust your words, darling, he says.

"Yeah! I am aware of that" she says, with charming smile.

Despite, the series of the situations, that hindered them, not to act in love. Sami gets too busy to enjoy her beauty.

"You invaded my thoughts, filled with love my heart and my mind".

She surprises herself, with a loving smile. "I love you". He moves to hug and kiss her. "I love you Saba".

"I hope I will be the woman… you deserve!"

"Honey!"… "After all I awe you", he says, trying to pull him closer to her chest.

Tripoli city.

A terrible strong desert wind, raising dust to the sky, hobbles over the area, completely turning it to look foggy. The Lead Trafficker, with his cellphone on his hand, calls the Boat Man in Tripoli, to get ready for the trip. He instructs him to take care of Sami and his men.

"Hello! Hello!"

"I am sending you 12 passengers".... "Please don't charge them, and don't ask them for a tip.

"Why?"

"Because they saved my life from the evil ISIS". "Did you get them, all those damned ISIS".

"If it was not, through the mighty, east African fighters, my life was at death risk".

Only five hours drive remains to reach their destination Tripoli City. Throughout the long drive, on the Sahara desert, on their way, all are relaxed and in a happy mood. They chat loudly, almost to forget, the hate feeling, against the Rashaida and the Bedouin. In the middle, suddenly, Saba wakes up from her deep sleep.

"Where are we?" she asks, kind of low voice, staring at Sami. He gives her a feedback look.

"Ask my friend Jobe, for he is wonderful fellow, in locating places".

Jobe, turns his face to Saba.

"Few miles to reach our destination."

Sami's eyes search from a distant, the tip of the high-rise building of the city Tripoli. Bright lights twinkles, crowed the horizon. All are awake from their sleep, not talking, but staring at each other, in dark. It'll take them fifteen minutes drive, just to reach their destination. Saba, blinks, to see out if all is real.

"Oh... God" Saba says, turning her face, yawning. Sami holds his breath for seconds.

"Baby, I like your snoring! You are a champion", he says. She laughs in a low tone.

"A champion! A champion! What do you mean, Honey?" Sami teasingly, chuckles.

"The rhythm of your snoring, follows exactly the beat, of Jobe's krar songs".

Tries to be serious, for whatever it's. "Please don't tease me", Sami.

Changes the subject. "Any way did you dream?" Saba sighs.

"How can I dream?"... "When an overwhelming noise, dominate my mind".

Sea Shore.

Finally, they reach their destination. Before they are to proceed, to cross the Mediterranean Sea, all stay near the Sea shore. Some of them relax sitting under a wooden roof, while other go swimming, on the shallow water.

Saba and Lula are on their own, sitting on the beach and watching the group swimming. Lula, her mind shifting into celebrating mood, leans towards Saba ears.

"All the way I was kind worried, about the unborn baby of our hero".

Saba, holds her hands resting protectively, on her belly.

"If I am healthy, he too is healthy! I hope, all our horrible experience, of life and death ends here and now".

The thing that every individual of the group, are thinking draws to one and dangerous issue, that of crossing the Mediterranean Sea. Lula's eyes turn to the water, seeing Sami swim like a professional, swimming back and forth.

"Wow", she says, excitedly and smiling at her.

"It's kind of cute, for Sami, to show his swimming skill, she adds.

"He better be" Saba replies, her mind not dismissing his heroism. Both enjoy the view, chatting about the awful experience of an escape from their beloved land.

Sami's enjoying swimming on the deep water, while Jobe, is trying to swim on the shallow. When Sami gets tired swimming, he joins Jobe, both standing in the shallow water.

"You swim good, Sami! Where did you learn to swim?" Jobe asks.

"Not, like the professional swimmers though", Sami replies.

"Where did you learn it", he asks. "Really you were having fun swimming" he adds.

"I learned it swimming at Lake Shifshifit", he responds. Jobe squints at him.

"Well, it's something than nothing! At least you save your life, swimming in case...

"In case of what?" Sami asks.

"God forbid!"... "I mean if we get in trouble, in the middle of the sea", he responds.

All sleep on the ground, exhausted from the tough and rough drive on the desert. The cold weather, wouldn't let them sleep well. Sami, sits in sitting position, as Saba lies down, on top of Sami's thigh. In the middle of the night, suddenly, Saba's phone rings. It's her Mom, Anna on line.

Saba, never tries to pick it up. Again, several times it rings, finally, Sami to respond.

"Hello!", She says, a male voice to hear.

"Hello" responds Sami, in a low voice, not to wake Saba, from her sleep.

"Are you Sami?" Anna asks. Sami, puts her on hold.

In the middle Saba wakes up. Her eyes becomes red, because of oversleep. Tries to sit in a sitting position", wiping her face with her hand. Sami, puts his hand on her forearm, handing the phone to Saba.

"Hello" says Saba, her voice trailing off. "Where're you now? Anna asks.

Saba doesn't know the exact place.

"We're at...." Pauses for seconds, looking at Sami, sideway, wiping her lower eyes, with her finger.

Sami tries to tell Saba the exact location, in a whisper leaning against her ear.

"Tripoli" in Libya. "Triboli" Anna echoes.

"Wait! Wait!"... "Let me ask your Grandpa" Anna says, holding her on hold.

Her eyes widely opened, asks about the location to Grandpa. He's well acquainted with the place, since he physically was present there, during World war two, fighting against the British, being Italian soldier.

"Now I know where exactly, you're" Anna says, after the brief feed back from Grandpa.

Anna pats her hands on her chest, feeling good to meet her daughter.

Anna, again being on line, her tone low, asks, about the escape from the desert prison cells.

"All over the country, the news of the the bravery escape, is diffused",... "Where you in that incidence?"

Saba, gazes at Sami's, smiling widely. "Yes we were".

"It's Sami who broke the prison, to let us, all free". She adds.

"I don't doubt on Sami's bravery".

"I know, his urine and the green paper, with his gut, it really worked."

"You're very lucky, under God, to have a brave husband." Both hang up their phones.

After spending, almost half hour chatting, her eyes focusing, in the view of the desert, looks at Sami sideways. Sighs. "I wish Mom understands our situation?" Sami refrains, from saying anything, not showing in his face, the sign of fear.

Saba, fears thoughtfully, of the worst things, that can happen.

"As God saved us, from the Bedouin jaw, he'll save us, from the Mediterranean Sharks.

Sami, "Nods".

60PART FIVE.

The Sea voyage.

All wake up from their sleep, early in the morning, sitting in a circle, enjoying the local cultural songs, from an old tape-recorder, being in the middle. Everyone, is busy, re- visiting in their mind, all the horrors of their voyage, turning their experience into a memory. Sami, sneaks out from the group and steps towards, the Boat Man.

The Boat man, is busy, preparing and arranging for the trip, checking the engine and the other parts of the small motor boat, smoking cigarette. The Boat Man, senses some one's on top of him, not knowing, who it's. One more time, moves his head up, just to see, Sami, standing over him.

"What will the weather be tomorrow?" Sami asks. Makes a direct eye contact.

"Not the right person to ask! My dear". "Why?"

"Not graduated in weather forecasting".

"I hear you! Let us try our chance", Sami responds.

Sami walks back, stepping towards his group. While on his way, his cell phone rings. His uncle Hailu's on the other end calling from Germen. Sami picks the call.

"Hello!" he answers, not knowing the caller, sounding a male. "Hello!" He says, "this's Hailu, your uncle"...

The sound of ShShSh buzzes on Sami's ear, unable to identify the caller. "I'm Hidru your uncle" again he shouts.

"Sami speaking", he responds.

The news of an escape from the Bedouin prison jails, is diffused, through the social media channels, though not knowing Sami's part of the story.

Embarrassed smeared with fear.

"Where you there at the time?" Sami interrupts him. "What did you hear? He asks.

"I just heard about the breaking of the Bedouin prison cells, by brave Eritreans" he answers.

Sami gets quiet for seconds. "I'm in the news you have heard".

He clears his throat. "Okay, I want you to tell me what happened".

"Do you deserve that much?" Sami asks. "Yes I do", he answers promptly.

"I just saved my life", Sami ventures, really wanting to get off the phone.

He chuckles. "The main character in the action? "You said it".

"I feel proud of you". "How did you do it?"

"I made a home made plastic bomb". "Then".

"I mixed in a plastic bottle, my urine with a green paper powder.

"And then".

"I splash it, on the face of the Bedouin Guard.

Their conversation terminate because of bad connections.

Half-hour later.

The survivors of the desert, get into a heated chat, not arguing, just sharing their reflections, life under the Bedouin prison cells. Sami's out for the time being, meeting with the Boat Man. All're twenty yards away, from the motor- boat. Half an hour later, Sami steps towards his group.

Stands, still before them, ready with the instruction, to deliver them. All keep silent, ready to hear from Sami.

"Everything is ready guys" he pronounces.

"The only remaining enemy, is the Sea" he adds.

All remain silent, each hiding their fears. Sami, leaves them for a moment, stepping towards Saba, who's sitting alone at the corner. Reading the expression on her face:-

"I hope you're ready for the next journey, he says, focusing his attention, one more time, to the danger of the sea.

"How long will it take us to cross the sea" she asks, feeling perplexed.

He tries to tell her what he knows.

"Maybe between twelve-twenty four hours", he says, not bothered to give her an answer.

Whispering into Sami's ear, sits down, looking him directly in his eyes. Smiles, lightly scratching her lower body.

"Honey I am glad! That the baby is yours".

Sami, grins. "The merit is yours, I am glad to be your husband".

Saba, holds his hands tightly.

"Don't you see! Everyone is so proud of you?" Before he's to answer she gives him a kiss.

"Never get stressed honey, forget the assassin Bedouin, like your mother feeding breasts", she says.

Still, coming into his mind, the merciless Bedouin images, a reality he has not learned to accept, he says, "Heroes don't live! It is their history that is inherited".

Few minutes later.

Boat Man honks several honks, as all the group start walking towards the shore. He orders all to board, in a high tone, curving his hands like a cone, putting against his mouth.

"Get aboard! Get aboard".

Saba and Sami keeping their line, they board on the boat 15 by 6 yard, all together with all the passengers being more than 350 people. The boat is overcrowded, no enough space to walk, besides sitting down on the deck.

The boat wobbling its way out, it starts to navigate, on the Mediterranean Sea, heading towards the small Island, of Lampedusa in Italy. Sami, sits between Saba and his friend Jobe. Sami, delicately caresses her hair and leans against her shoulder.

In a whisper, "You look so beautiful today, darling".

Saba, touches her hair and feels so grateful, for his up lifting comment. Smiles. "But my hair is not well done, honey".

"I understand of what you say", he responds.

Saba, feels more at ease, curving O' shape her lips, ready to give him a kiss.

"You look nice too".

Sami, chuckles. "Everybody is going to be looking at you, instead of the ocean".

Saba, "I wish I am on my own".

Both of them laugh and share glances, at each other. Jobe, catching up with their discussion.

"I am beginning, to wish you a good wish", he says in a whisper tone.

Wedding ring.

The boat is moving smoothly, for several hours. All seem settled in silence. Sami, stands still in the middle of all, as all eyes focus on him. Turns his face towards Saba, with a big smile. He invites her to step towards him, remaining standing, ready to surprise her, that she's not ready, mentally. Saba, accepts his invitation, not knowing anything, standing before him. With a ring of engagement in his hand, suddenly, he kneels down before Saba. Takes out a ring. All are, curiously observing the show. He puts the ring on Saba's finger.

"Oh dear," she breaths quietly, her tears ready to come out, in drips. She feels a strong feeling, this time about the surprise. Sami, pronounces in low voice.

"I'll be your husband, till death separates us".

Saba, cries with emotion. She bows down, holding his two hands, attempting to raise him up.

Me too, I'll be your wife, till death separates us", she echoes.

A middle-aged Woman, raises her voice with the cultural expression of "Elilta".

"As we are testifying, right now your engagement. May God give us, the health and strength, to join you, in your child's birth", she expresses.

A sound of applause rains, none stop, from all the passengers.

Middle of the Sea.

Saba, feeling a feeling of fatigue, for the long journey, lays her head, on Sami's thigh, falling into a deep sleep. All memories, of her love experience, while at Sawa training camp, in a dream spells out, as she is deeply snoring.

Sami wakes her up by kissing her lips. Saba, Comes back to the reality.

"Where are we, Honey?"

"Right now we are, in the middle of the Sea". She sighs gently.

"Me, I was in the other world".

"You mean in the world of dreams", he responds.

"Exactly! Dreaming about our life in Sawa camp, the military training", she says, smiling, at her awed expression.

"Good or bad?" he asks.

"It's only, my dream feeling, but really I don't know" she says.

On the other end of the boat, Two Young males, Feden and Fanus, entertain an argument, discussing, about their bad military experiences, at Sawa military camp.

In the middle, they enter into a political discussion. Feden, voices.

"I'm fed up, for how long you will speak, about this Sawa.

"It's our life my dear! Despite our bad experience", Fanus suggests.

Feden, not looking okay:-

"I doubt, if the world knows about our problems, of escaping the country".

Fanus discredits the issue of their escape.

"If our own regime, disregard our problem!"... "What do you expect from the world?"

Feden stares at him, for seconds, in an interrupt mood.

"I feel bad!"... "I am tired of all this none sense, old politics".

On the corner of the boat, two young Girlfriends, Senu and Fallen are discussing their wedding experience, while back home. The boat is moving in a slow motion and all are relaxed.

"How was your wedding back home, Fallen?" Senu asks, hiding her excitement for a moment.

"It was gorgeous, my friend", responds Fallen. Not to go into a detail, she just hands, her wedding photo album.

Senu, looks at her side way, focusing her views on the album. Goes all through her album, while Fallen, puts all her attention, viewing the sea. Total silence reigns between them. Fallen on her part, gets eager to hear from her, about her wedding. Rolls her eyes and looking at her friend sideways.

"How was your wedding? She inquires. "Very amazing!" Senu responds.

"Did you ride a limo?" She asks curiously. "To your surprise, our limo was a camel".

"Really, I can't believe it" she says breathing lightly.

"I wish my wedding was same like yours", she says, giving her a full look, smiling.

"I wish we survive the sea, to share more about our experiences", Senu replies.

Six hours later.

After the cold night on the boat, the sun begins to rise from the East. All are awake, still in deep silence worried about their fate. Sami, gets sick of sitting and steps towards the sailor man, who is smoking a big cigar in a relaxed mood.

Backs his head away, trying not to look at Sami, emitting a big puff to the air.

"Unique wedding on the Sea", the Sailor says, his eyes dove from his face to his belly.

Your first engagement? He adds, touching his lips with his fingers.

A stiffness forms around his mouth, as Sami eyes him.

"Well you are not allowed to know, all that".... "By the way are we near to our destination?"

Blinks at him for seconds, smiling weakly as he puffs out the smoke.

"Yes we are near".... "I hope the mother nature behaves to our advantage" responds swallowing hard, not showing his feelings.

When only three miles remain, to reach their destination Lampedusa Island, another bad and very strong wave, hits the boat, making it swerve back to the opposite direction. Steps towards the boat man and stands before him, in a tormented look on his eyes.

"Stop the engine! Stop the engine!"... The boat is moving towards the opposite direction".

All cry loud and shout, for the fear of not drowning.

The boat man, hurries around the corner of the wheel and stops the engine. The boat stops moving, as the chaos and low moral of the passengers cools down.

Saba clearly terrified, is sitting on the deck, not changing an inch from her position. Sami, steps back to her and sits on the floor, landing his legs onto her legs.

Pauses and looks at him, blinking her eyes a little confused about the danger.

"Honey! From that one, huh, this one is worse".... "I mean we have hard time at Sinai desert under the Bedouin, but I doubt, if we can ever survive this Sea.

Tries to give her a moral feedback, narrowing his eyes at her.

"I know how hard it was, to be under the horrible Bedouin prisons.

In his mind, reads the harsh treatment of the Bedouin.

"Don't destroy your mind, since God's actions are unreachable. Now is time, only to focus on our journey for our safe trip.

The boat proceeds to sail, on the right direction, towards their destination. Few minutes later, all hear another big crackle, that starts slowly, getting louder and louder.

The sailor, as he hears, the crackling sound again, this time, gets nervous. He sneaks down to the motor cabin, with tools in his hands.

Half a minute later, he steps back to the wheel, again restarting the engine. Sami heads back stepping towards Sailor again.

For a while, they stay holed up, in the middle of the sea. All on board, begin to get panicked and shocked. The Sailor, waves his hands on the air and desperately announces to all the passengers, about the problem of the engine.

"Calm! Calm! It is not very serious, just stay calm!"

Silence dominates to all the passengers. All enter into a deep thought, in a speechless condition, for the fear of not drowning into the sea, to feed the Mediterranean Sharks.

Saba, falls all her body onto Sami's, holding his hand tight, all her body trembling.

"Are we going to die!"

Sami, though he pretends to be calm, he can't avoid his fear, as he puts his arm, around Saba's shoulder.

"Calm! Calm!" In silence blaming himself, for all these tragic moment.

The boat proceeds, navigating. All they see's a cloudless sky and the blue water, surrounding them.

Half an hour later, the boat again encounters, another big wave, floating it left and right rapidly. All get panicked.

The boat man, struggles to manage the boat, under all the pressure and odd circumstance, slightly smiling unwanted smile.

Saba all distressed, is absorbed by the danger of the water. Sami follows the situation, in the unnatural stillness mood, but not showing to Saba.

She approaches Sami, as a state of agony flows into her mind.

"Sami, Sami, can you do something to save us from this dumb Sea?

"Not this time."... "You are imploring to the wrong person." "Lord" she says, getting irritated all over again.

"Sorry this time I'm limited."... "I can't fight with nature."

Within a short distance of the second departure, half a mile to reach their destination, again the motor of the boat, starts to emit a big smoke, which later it turned to be a big fire. The passengers run in panic and to avoid the fire, one after the other they start to dive to the water. Sami holding her hand tight, struggles to the end, then both dive to the water swimming.

As Sami is a professional swimmer and with an athletic body, he starts to drag Saba, by her hair swimming fast towards the shore.

Sami leaves Saba on a safe place, on the shore. Suddenly, as he turns his face, towards the water, he sees his best friend Jobe, from a deep water, waving his arm for help. Again leaves Saba on the shore, giving her a kiss.

"You stay here! You stay here!"

Dives to the water, to save his friend Jobe, as Saba follows Sami to the shallow water edge.

The rescue ship.

A big Italian rescue ship and dozens of small boats, sail in and around the shore, of the Lampedusa Island. They get busy, loading the cadavers of almost 365 victims; one by one putting them in a casket and labeling each casket, by numbers until they find their identity, from their ID's and passports.

On the scene, there are more than 50 medical crew members, more than 100 military Personals and many volunteers. The medical crew give assistance to the survivors and the military help collect the dead victims.

Two Military Men, carry on a stretcher, a female survivor, behind them a Nurse's following them, side by side with the infusion bag on her right hand.

Military One, in a whisper tone talks to the nurse, his mouth covered by a mask.

"It really is a disaster."... "To avoid back home death, they encounter another death."

Military Two, feels like a desolate, looking at the female on the stretcher, side way.

"Before they reach the unknown land, to end up, at the Sharks belly!

Saba looks towards the sea, expecting the safe return of Sami and his friend Jobe. Thirty minutes later, she feels hopeless and helpless when she sees no sign of Sami's return from the water. She feels that she lost her sweetheart. A strange silence fell, as Saba is sitting down, on the ground.

Her right-hand moves from side to side, with her eyes narrowed, to see what she can see. After waiting for quite time, she starts to cry and shout. Only hears her echo, repeatedly bombarding her mind.

"Heroes don't live! It is their act that's inherited! She smacks onto the ground, yelling.

"Sami! Sami! Sami."

Unable to take her eyes off the sea, beats her chest crying and screaming loudly.

"Did the Mediterranean Sharks, swallow you?" Again throws herself to the ground.

"I can't face the danger alone again."

She gets up from the ground, shouting with a fainted voice. "Did you betray me! Sami! Sami!"

Saba, steps back some yards away from the shore, sitting on a stone under the tree, as a thick dark cloud surrounds the area. Feels apart for the loss of her husband and looks upward crying in a fainted voice.

"I will miss you forever".... "I am not ready to face this danger."... "Without you, no life to live Sami".

Calling his name, bows her head down, facing to the ground, as tears run down her face.

Again rubbing her womb gently, looks upward, to the clouds.

"The baby boy that I carry, will be named after you."... "The lion of the Sea".

At Lampedusa open market place, a Homeless Man, mid sixty, wearing old and tattered cloths', is preaching and prophesying in the middle of the market.

"It's our fault and the fault of our father's".... "And don't blame, for all these horrific scenes, of mass migrations, to the poor people of Africa".

An Old Woman, "To whom are you pointing your finger" she asks, looking fixedly at his eyes.

Boldly, faces at her.

"My complaint is to you and like you"-. She interrupts him.

"What're you talking about?" She asks. Rolls his eyes.

"Since you are white and European, the blame falls on you, my dear".

"How?"

"You are part of the white generation, that colonized the continent of Africa".

"So!"

"I only tell you! I'll never force you, to swallow the truth".

Two Fishermen, on their way doing their daily duty, they see a big fire in the middle of the sea. As they approach near the burning fire, they learn that a boat is under fire.

Suddenly, the two fishermen only 10 feet distant, from their boat, they see a body of unborn baby, still attached with his mother umbilical cord, both dead floating on the sea.

The two fishermen dive, to recover the dead bodies. Cover the bodies, with a white blanket, tears running down his cheeks.

"Alas! This the end of the world!"

Moves his head right and left, feeling the feeling of anger.

"What sin did the unborn infant baby, committed?... "Whom to blame under the sky?"

Sami, is struggling, to save his best friend Jobe, from drowning. After several minutes, he gets tired and tries to save himself, swimming back towards the shore. When he sees the fishermen from a distant, he raises his head up from the water and waves his hand.

"Help! Help!"

Fisherman One, glances over from his boat, to see hand waving to the air. Real quick, diverts the direction of the boat, towards Sami.

"I see, a hand of a drowning human, waving".

Fisherman Two, his body starts to shake, watching that ease cross his face.

"I hear you! Let us speed up!"

Lampedusa shore.

A white STRANGER WOMAN on her sixty's from Lampedusa Island, walks from the other side of the shore, barefoot on the beach. As she sees Saba from distant, she steps towards her approaching her from behind.

Saba didn't see her, until she comes near to her. Feeling agonizingly, struggling to concentrate in her mind, as she senses a human presence, instantly Saba glances at her. The Stranger Woman, greets Saba in a low voice.

"Hi! Hi! What are you doing here?"... On your own here.

Her eyes, appearing to have sunk into their sockets, in tears waves her hand weakly, as she is not able to speak.

"I just survived from the sea".

The Stranger Woman, as she looks towards the sea, she sees a dying fire with a big smoke, making a dark cloud around.

"I see you are the survivor! What is your name?"

Saba, feels her heart pounding, out of grief, moving her head towards her from where she sat.

"Saba! Saba!" She repeats.

Forwards to her a courtesy look with a smile. "Wonderful name! And you look so beautiful.

Saba and the Stranger Woman, walk down a narrow street heading towards the house of the White Lady. Suddenly, Saba feels sick, because of the long walk and being pregnant. She looks over her womb rubbing it with her hand, after which she sits on the street side. The Stranger Woman, sits beside her leaning close to her.

"Are you not feeling good?"

Regime's reaction to the tragedy.

The sole TV, run by the regime, late in the morning begins to broadcast, in its news session, about the daily program. A female news caster, shows up, wearing a white traditional dress "Zuria", sitting on decorated platform. She starts to recite the local and world news for quite time, at the end, the final minutes, to mention the tragedy of Lampedusa.

Here's the brief content of the news she transmitted. "Several Africans while attempting to cross the Mediterranean Sea have being drown onto the water", she says, tactically hiding, not covering the truth of the incident.

Asli and Anna were at their respective home, both following the news. After the brief message of the news, Asli, picks her cell phone and dials to Anna. Anna's getting ready to go shopping for the day. Her phone rings several times, before she picks it up.

"Did you follow the news on TV?" Asli sighs.

"Yes I did", responds not saying anything for seconds. "Very bad news".

"I don't know, Asli, she says.... "Just I don't know what to say".

"I'm kind worried about Saba and Sami"...." They could be victims of this tragedy".

"Spit it out, Asli."

Her whole body seems to sigh. She pauses. "May our children survive with the survivors".

"I'm confused about the bad news, we heard from the TV."

"She just said it, as life never even mattered"...." Like life never meant anything to her".

Three hours after the tragedy.

Anna riding a horse cart she goes to the marketplace. Upon returning from the marketplace, holds her head low and manages to maintain, the sad news of the tragedy, breathing deep. Suddenly, her cell phone rings. She slumps down on the carts wooden seat. Jumps to the street, to answer the phone, leaving all her grocery on the cart.

"Hello! Hello!" she repeats in a loud voice.

Saba immersed in a deep thought, she feels terrified to tell her mother about the tragedy.

"It's me Saba talking",... "how're you mom?"

Saba's using the cell phone of the white lady. That's why her Mom was not able to recognize the caller. Once she made sure who's on the other end of the line, she starts keep talking.

"Nice to hear from you". She says, feeling a sudden shock, changing her phone, from right to the left ear.

Anna, mutters, struggling to her feet.

"How about you?" Saba shrugs, apparently having exhausted her say.

"I'm fine despite your absence". Anna says, struggling to keep her voice calm.

"Where're you now?"

Covers her mouth with her hand, to cover her groan.

"Actually, right now I am on the Island of Lampedusa, in Italy". She mouths in a whisper tone.

As she hears the name Lampedusa, her mind starts to crash within the reality, of the news earlier she heard. Pulls her sleeves up ward, adjusts her phone to her ear.

"Where's this Lampedusa? She asks, eagerly waiting for the response.

"In Italy".

Not feeling comfortable, "Do you mean the place where the tragedy happened? Anna asks.

Her tone becomes, decidedly weaker and weaker. "Is Sami with you?"

Saba, gets intrigued by her mom's question. After a brief silence, she gasps.

"No! No mom. He is not with me".

Changes her phone, from one side of her ear to another, frightened by the bad news, her hands trembling.

"So where is he?"

Feels a very strange sensation in her mind, as she suddenly finds herself.

"I lost my precious husband".

She punches in a fist hand to her left hand. "Tell me what really happened to him?

Pauses for seconds, as a stream of tears, flow down her cheeks.

"He's not with me anymore. I don't know, he might be dead!

Afflicted by the bad news, closes her eyes stream of tears flowing down her cheeks.

He's dead! He's dead! But how?"

"After he saved me from the sea, he hugged me and left me alone, to save his best friend Jobe.

Sobs and cries in a low voice.

"Since I never see him come back, I guess so".

Returns to the horse cart. Before she is to hang-up her phone, still tears streaming down her cheeks, her heart none stop hammers.

"What bad news? It's not what we have been waiting for, all those days and months."..." They escaped to save their lives from the Tiger's land",... "to be victims, the food for the Mediterranean Shark".

Saba cries loudly, holding her cell phone in her right hand and rubbing her tears from her eyes.

Emergency room.

The two fishermen after trying with their first aid to help Sami, they rush to the nearest hospital, on the island of Lampedusa, as he is breathing slowly.

About five doctors follow Sami, as he lays in the emergency room. Sami's Semi-conscious, almost in a status of coma.

Three Doctors and several Nurses surround him, with their white robes. All leave the room, except the Lead Doctor and a Female Nurse, remaining behind.

The Lead Doctor, leans forward, towards the bed. He looks deep into Sami's eyes and checks his pulses.

"He has a good chance of surviving", he says, Looking at Nurses face.

She nods.

The Nurse stands, beside the cart, with all the medical tools.

"I hope so", she adds.

Rubs his temple and stretches his hand across his eyes, stepping towards the Nurse.

"He is so weak he needs an infusion to give him strength". "Nods".

The nurse gets busy, setting all the medical tools, as the Doctor walks out, into the hall.

White Lady's home.

One mile apart, on the other part of the Island, Saba is staying in a small room alone, with the White Lady; who hosted her, to live with her in her apartment.

Weakened by the successive tragedy one after the other. "God! You throw us out of our beloved country.

"How can I do my life without Sami my husband?"

Reviews all her life in distress, in silence, one time bowing her head down and one time raising her head.

"Poor children of my nation!"... "If one is only lucky, one can do it. As, for me I am not lucky".

Not moving from where she is sitting, glances out of indifference. Suddenly, she sees through her window, a colony of white pigeons, flying over the sky.

The White Lady, after she prepares the breakfast, she sets down the table by placing forks, spoons and plates.

Steps, towards the room of Saba and slightly knocks the door. "Breakfast is ready come and join me gentle lady".

Saba follows her footsteps, slowly stepping towards the dining room. She sits down on a chair, facing her, across the table. Both look at each other, as Saba frowns like her chair gotten too hard to sit in.

The White Lady, notices Saba's body reaction, she gives her a touch on the shoulder, keeping her eyes straight onto her, to make her more comfortable.

"You are lucky enough to get out from the burning fire alive".... "I hope your husband is among the survivors".

Saba, rubs the back of her neck, tears flowing down her cheeks, feeling not to recite, all the dramatic stories of survival.

"I got out of it safe and alive but I lost my beloved husband".

The White Lady, sees on her face, reading a sign of despair. Invites her, to consume the last remaining food, on the table.

"Here you have, eat my baby".

Saba, starts to eat, as the sensation of her hunger fades, she opens her eyes.

"Thank you!"

Saba sits on the Sofa. She starts to admire the generosity and good gesture of the White Lady. Her mind destroyed from the race of all the anxiety, she looks up towards the ceiling.

The White Lady leaves her alone. Saba in a silence, revisits all her love life with Sami; the crucial war situation and the Bedouin prison cells at Sinai desert.

A week after the tragedy.

The White Lady walks to the hospital, to check out if Saba's husband, by chance is among the survivors. Walks through the main entrance gate and rushes towards the Patients board to read the name of all the survivors.

A female Clerk, on the front desk, is busy arranging files of the patients. Licking her lipstick lips, raises her head giving her little handshake with a smile.

"Hello there!"... "May I help you?"... "What're you looking for?"

Takes a deep breath, lowering her head from up down.

"I would like to know, if there is any survivor, by the name Sami".

The Clerk, looks into the file, to find the name. After few seconds she reads the name of a survivor, by name Sami.

"Yes he is one of the survivors, but right now, he is still unconscious and no one is allowed to visit him".

The White Lady, backs down stepping the corridor, towards the exit door, feeling a feeling of a relief.

Room 404.

Sami is recovering, though weak he slightly regains his consciousness. The Nurse pushing the medical cart, walks down the corridor with all the medicines. As she enters into the room, she starts to adjust the monitoring instruments.

Checks his heart beat and his breath as Sami gets a little conscious.

"Good morning!"..." Handsome survivor".... "Welcome back to the real planet". He unveils his face from the white sheet cover, a weak smile blossoming from his face.

"Where am I? He says, looking confused, about his where about.

"What really happened to me?" he adds.

Hands him a plastic thermometer, to insert it under his tongue.

"You were dead and now alive".... "If you are not dead, still you are breathing and healthy".

Gives him some tablets, with glass of water on her right hand.

"You were in the unconscious world, but now to the world of reality".

The Lead Doctor shows up, as Sami and the Nurse are discussing. He steps slowly, towards Sami's bed and leans at his bed. Shakes Sami's hand and greets him, glancing at the Nurse.

He, faces towards the nurse and stares at her, getting connected with all her work performances.

"Good job! Good Job!" he says. Again, looks at Sami, smilingly.

"Everything is alright, all medical results are okay"....

"After one week, you will be out of the hospital".

"Thank you for saving my life".

White Lady's home.

Saba is alone in the house, reciting in her mind the last scene of the tragedy. In her mind the case of Sami's existence, is a dead issue, since he left her swimming to save his friend. She is not aware, of Sami's being rescued by the fishermen.

The White Lady, as she assures the name of Sami, she walks down the street, stepping in a hurry, to tell Saba the good news of her husband, Sami. Steps, through the door, stepping towards Saba to tell the good news.

"I'm back, to tell you, the good news".... "I saw his name, on the files of the hospital".... "By the way "is your husbands name Sami? She asks.

She nods.

"Luckily, he's one of the survivors".... "I hope he is your husband", she adds.

Not being quite sure to believe the White lady, gazes at her in disbelief.

"What's the good News?"... "For me it's only an empty hope, as the sun doesn't rise, from the west".

Starts to punch her palm with her hand, in a slow rhythm.

"What do you mean by that?" Gives her a smirk as she whips her head around.

"In my mind, I mean my husband is dead".

Room 404.

The Lead Doctor, steps in to Room 404. He starts to perform, a routine checkup, before Sami is to be discharged. The Nurse is tidying the bed, as Sami is sitting on a sofa, now and then gazing at the Nurse with a smile.

The Nurse, grabs his arms and looks at him, in the eyes with a wide smile.

"It's so nice to finally see you healthy and alive".

Sami, stands before her there blinking, as he lowers his voice.

"Very nice, to have me, being assisted by all of you".

"By the way did you come all the way from Africa, by yourself?"

Bows, his head down to the floor, taking a deep breath.

"No, but I was together with my wife and hundreds of my country people".

"I understand I hope your wife will be among the survivors". Again, he drops his eyes to the floor.

"The last things I remember about my wife is, when I was dragging her swimming to the shore".... "That's my last recollection I have'.

The Nurse, tries not get into more serious questions, to give him hard time and pounds, her way out of the room.

Half an hour later, both, Saba and the White Lady, rush towards the hospital, riding a taxi. While they are in the taxi, Saba once again to make sure, she asks her about the good news she heard. Glances at her in disbelief.

"Did you see him?"... "How does he look like?" Slightly, distances in her voice, smiling warmly at her face.

"I hope I kiss your good news. If ever my husband survives, with the survivors".

Sami, is waiting for the last remaining check-ups, before he is to be discharged from the hospital. The Nurse, extends the thermometer, towards his mouth.

"How are you feeling today?"

Uncovers his head, by taking away the white sheet from his head.

"Great! Great!"

The nurse pulls the medical cart, towards Sami's bed, just to perform her routine checkups.

On their way, Saba and the White Lady, step towards a booth to get their name batch. A Clerk, greets them as they near to the counter booth. The Clerk tucks, her dark hair, behind her ears, giving to both a diplomatic smile, sitting in front of big screen.

"May I have the patient's name, that you are about to visit". Saba, steps forward, as the White Lady, stays where she is. "His name is Sami".

Opens the file and as she reads, the exact name, on the computer, she takes a tag name and gives to both, keeping her head high as she smiles.

"Go to room 404".

Both, step fast, on the long corridor, of the hospital.

The Nurse, closes the door, leaving Sami alone, in room 404. She walks out stepping down the corridor, pushing the medical cart.

From the opposite side of the corridor, from distant she sees Saba and the Strange Woman, rushing down the corridor.

In the middle of the corridor, she stands still, glancing at them curiously. Suddenly, she intervenes politely, stepping several yards towards them.

"May I help you?"

The White Lady, smiles.

"If we are at the right place, we want to visit a patient in room 404".

Holds the cart and glances at both with a smile. "You are here! "What's the name of the patient".

Saba, stares into her eyes, and returns a weak smile to the nurse.

"Sami! Sami!"

The Nurse, notices the name and points out, towards the room, from distant.

"Right destination!" Gazes at Saba with a smile. "Beauty! Are you related with the patient, in room 404?" "If ever, the one I am looking for, is my husband".

Blinks her eyes and smiling widely. "Really!

"Okay, let me surprise him and then you complete the surprise".

The Nurse walks back to room 404. Saba and the White Lady remain standing, waiting outside behind the door.

She leaves the cart on the corridor and opens Sami's bedroom, walking towards Sami, in a tip-toe. Smiles at Sami's face, in her mind getting impressed about the situation.

"Surprise! Surprise! Mr. Sami.... "I have good news for you. Your wife Saba is here".

Sits straight on his bed, as he hears the surprise, trying to put his legs on the floor.

"May I taste the surprise!

May the Angels of our country, kiss your mouth".

The Nurse, opens the door wide and looks up through the corridor. With her pointing finger, invites them to come in.

Sami sees Saba walking through the door. Out of joy he starts to sing. Quickly, he goes down from his bed and dances around twisting on the floor. Feels a thrill of excitement. "I can't believe it!"

In a slow motion, Saba carrying a bunch of flowers on her right-hand steps towards him. Sami steps towards Saba, as both hug and kiss each other for quite time. She raises both of her hands to the air.

"Thank God!"... "For opening the safety door for me"

"I am feeling a wonderful of hope".... "Right now my soul is celebrating happiness".

Few hours later, Sami is discharged from the hospital.

Sami and Saba walk down the corridor, hand in hand as the White Lady, follows their footsteps. In the middle, Saba's cell phone rings. It's her mother from back home, that is online. Saba did not pick the phone, until it finished ringing, though Sami advises her to respond the call.

She hears her cell phone ringing several times. Sami touches her arm as they walk side by side.

"Who's calling you?"

She is not willing to pick the phone as her mind runs none stop, to make things easy.

"It's Mom? I will call her back, when I'm done with the surprise".

"It is me and you honey".... "Let me enjoy you, for you were lost and found, dead and alive".

Again kisses and hugs Sami. "For almost a week, I have been trying, to find you among the dead".

Both walk side by side, embracing their hands, looking and glancing at each other, in a smile. As they reach the main gate of the Lobby, they move to the hospital exit counter table. After brief silence, they interact with The Clerk and both step towards the Exit gate.

Referring to the most impossible situations, of his being alive, he leans towards her body.

"I experienced the partial death, being unconscious, for almost three days".

"I hope the baby in your womb is healthy and alright".

Saba, in her mind silently processes the facts, separating the joy and the sadness she encountered, being immensely painful.

"If you are not dead, you are still alive".... "But…, back home you are still dead!"

Overtaken by the situation, he gazes at her in a surprised face.

"Still, dead! What did you tell them?"

"That you are drowned on the Mediterranean Sea".

The White Lady, joins them, slowly stepping towards Saba and Sami, expressing her joy to both of them.

Gazes and smiles at Saba.

"It is good that your wish is positively fulfilled".

With a clear face, Saba appreciates and thanks Sami, for his act of heroism.

"Blessed feet! God sent protector! At the time I was despaired, you were there for me, all the time".

The White Lady, stares at Sami in a smile. "Congratulations! Congratulations!"

Looks sideways, his eyes falling, onto the White Lady. "Thank you!"

"By the way! Who is she?"

Saba, smiles facing the face of the White Lady. She turns back her smile to Sami, recounting in her mind the benevolent and the personal help, she got from the Stranger Woman.

"She's the savior of the survivor's wife".

The surprise meeting of Sami and Saba, happened two weeks after the tragedy. On their way Sami, Saba and the White Lady, all ride on a taxi. Suddenly, Saba looks out through the taxi's window, enjoying the panorama and the beauty of the Island.

"What a gorgeous place it is! No one can give you unless you have chance".

Gets impressed, as he joins her impressions, glancing at her for long moment.

"Yeah, it is a paradise compared to our arid land".

The White Lady, comments, on the causes of, an unforeseen complication.

"To acquire the gold that you don't see, you lost the diamond you see'.

In a settled mind, looks at the situation sadly.

"Appreciate what you have, before diving into others"...." I hope your minds shop, the right way".

All go down from the taxi and walk towards the apartment of the White Lady. Suddenly, Saba stumbles. Sami picks her up, with his right hand, as she mentally curses herself in murmur.

"Right now, your mother is remembering you".

Saba, follows his say, with an attitude of curiosity, trying to stay on her feet, in Sami's hand.

"What's the relation of my stumbling, with my mother's remembrance?"

"You owe her a call, for an earlier missed-call!"... "Missed call might be a missed opportunity".

Pulls her hair off her face, still being under his arm, she smiles.

"Oh, Honey how sweet you are! I, almost forgot, to call my mom.

"I will call her right back".

Anna for all two weeks, never said or shared with any about the Lampedusa tragedy. She secretly organizes a spiritual and cultural celebration for a dead. Asli not knowing about it, joins the celebration. All the neighborhood families wearing a white and black cultural clothes sit under a big tent at Saba's house. Asli, gets confused, not having a clue, of whose death is remembered. An Elder Man from the neighborhood, raises from his seat. Standing, in front of all, he announces.

"Today we're all here to commemorate the death of "Sami". In the middle, Asli cries loudly, stepping left and right.

Tears run down her cheeks, attempting, to wipe it with her handkerchief.

"Not relieved yet from what I feared".... "I feel so horrible about the situation".... "It's so unfair, for my wonderful son Sami, to remain on the Sea"....

"Rather, he died in front of me", she voices, naturally not to accept the situation. Shakes her head in grief.

"Whom to blame? If not to curse, the main cause of their escape".... "Oh, the unknown dream, of the unknown land". Grinds her teeth together.

"Our little baked bread, would be enough and suffice, rather than their dream bread".

Suddenly, Anna's phone rings. She sees the caller's number and notices, it's her daughter calling. She steps out, trembling and shaking her hands. Picks up the phone. Over the phone.

"Hello! Hello! I am Saba! Calling".

"How are you mommy?" Attempts, to step further, out in a tip- toe.

"We are all fine!"... "Today we are fulfilling, the right for the dead, for Sami your husband".

Saba, backs up, few steps towards Sami and talks in a whisper, nearing towards his ear, keeping her mother on hold.

Covers the phone with both of her hands and leans towards Sami's right ear, talking in a whisper tone.

"Sami! Sami!"... "The dead and alive" she says, caught in between two realities".

Gets confused about the situation as both exchange uneasy look.

"What did you tell them?"

She pauses for seconds, venturing into the reality of what she communicated, earlier with her Mom.

"The reality of you being dead".

Saba turns back on the phone, to speak with her mother.

Jumps lightly on to the ground and in a very excited mood, she exchanges a love look at Sami.

"Mom! Mom!"... "Surprise!"... "The dead Sami is now alive!"

Repeats the words with her, still holding the phone on her ear in an excitement, checking her body.

"Alive! Alive! Alive! That's what I'm hearing?"

Her eyes fall, between holding the phone and staring at Sami.

"Yes Mom! He is alive! He is alive."

One time glancing at her phone, she remains astounded by the conversation with her daughter.

"I can't believe you! Let me talk to Sami, to hear his voice".

Hands the phone to Sami as she stands straight bowing down leaning against Sami's body.

"Here you have!"... "Talk to my mother!"... "The hero!"... "The savior of his wife".

Anna, in her mind, still fighting, with the reality, her whole body shakes and trembles.

"Hello! Your voice is Sami's!"... "But how can my mind compensate, to the earlier reality, of you being dead".

"This is Sami! Talking to you. I'm alive".

Suddenly, Anna runs towards all the neighborhood, who are gathered together, for Sami's cultural right for the dead with her open hand on the air, screaming in joy.

Lifts her both hands to the air and shouts out of joy in a loud voice.

"Stop! Stop! No mourning! No mourning!"

Not knowing of what is going on, Asli, stands on her feet. "What is going on? What is new?"

Anna, embraces Asli, giving her a cultural HUG and KISS, shouting a shout of joy.

"Let the mourning turn to celebration! For Sami the dead is alive".

As all hear the GOOD NEWS, they start to DANCE, with their DRUMS.

Sami and the White Lady, stand along the beach barefoot, both facing towards the Mediterranean Sea. Saba 6 month pregnant sits on a wooden bench.

In a relaxed mood, Saba glances at his face, with a big smile.

"Sami, Sami you are seen twice".... "I mean as dead and later to be alive".

A series of thoughts comes into his mind. He again and again glances at her face.

"Isn't that beautiful, isn't that wonderful, to get to see each other, to see your face again".

Gets quiet for a moment, feeling a rush of inexplicable relief.

"I love the fact, all we went through, the five tragedies, finally to earn the Surprise". Gets perplexed of what he said. Pauses for seconds,

"What're the five tragedies, you mention?

"All the tragedies, we passed through, on our way", he expresses.

"Can you spell them for me?" She asks.

"Okay",... "the tragedy of war",... "being kidnapped by the Rashaida",... "life under the Bedouin prison", "the desert battle with the ISIS and the Sea".... "Finally, to be turned in our favor".

The Lampedusa big Cathedral bells, are ringing in melody. The Mediterranean Sea, wave after wave, is agitating strongly.

Saba's last words "My hero the dead and alive" are scripted over a big shark swimming on the surface of the sea.

Saba exults in joy, in praise of Sami. "My hero the dead and alive". I can't believe it! Our tragic life turned to be a celebration of joy, just as we are sitting here alive and breathing. We are lucky to survive, but how many of our own country people, couldn't make it, to remain only to be the food for the MEDITERRANEAN SHARKS.

Sami, silently sits up straight, on a big rock and looks straight at Saba.

Saba steps towards him in a tip-toe, after which both EMBRACE, HUG and KISS each other.

On the book cover.

I sit on my seat, comfortably, in front of my computer. Back and forth with the old and new memories. It made so much sense. This time forget about "I", "We", I better wind down my story, with "He", "She" and "They". Changed my writing style, to make it more novel, rather than be a true story. In it's kind my writing performance, from my previous experiences, is completely different.

Brainstormed my mind, to title my project. Attempted, almost ten times. Here I come with number 5. The title is 5. Divided into 5. The whole content is not compiled in the past tense, but present tense, since the issue is still happening as I'm typing.

The novel is based, on a true experience of the people, I'm part of. My style follows more of a conversational dialogue. The main focus of my narrative, is centered on two Female Freedom fighters, who were buddies, in the armed struggle.